BUY AMERICAN

BUY THIS BOOK

BUY AMERICAN

BUY
THIS BOOK

Eric Lefcowitz

TEN SPEED PRESS
Berkeley, California

Ten Speed Press
P.O. Box 7123
Berkeley, California 94707

Cover design by Fifth Street Design
Book design and typography by Alex G. Mendoza

FIRST TEN SPEED PRINTING 1992

Library of Congress Cataloging in Publication Data
Lefcowitz, Eric.
    Buy American : buy this book / by Eric Lefcowitz.
      p. cm.
    ISBN 0-89815-495-2
    1. American wit and humor. 2. Buy national
      products—United States— Humor. I. Title.
PN6162.L373   1992
380.1'45—dc20
                               92-18554
                                  CIP
Printed in the United States of America

1 2 3 4 5 — 96 95 94 93 92

ACKNOWLEDGEMENTS

Anita Sethi
Alex G. Mendoza
Luis Piedrahita
Michael Ventura
Dan Simon
John Dolan
Jane Newman
Jeffrey Fiedler
Anne Wright
Sal Glynn
Mariah Bear
Phil Wood
Seymour Freedgood
Barbara Lefcowitz
Allan Lefcowitz
Uttam Sethi
Amrit Sethi
Bill Inglot
CU Library System
Matt Mates
Deborah Baldwin
Bob McElwaine
Marjorie Lefcowitz
Seth Feinberg
Kitty Bruce
Victor Marton
Stephen Escobar
Rebecca Peters
William J. Lynott
Michael Bennet
Andrew Sandoval
Quilter's Newsletter Magazine
Automotive News
The Buy American Foundation
        (PO Box 82, Abington, PA 19001)

TABLE
OF CONTENTS

INTRODUCTION

Are you a patriotic consumer? According to a recent Washington Post-ABC News poll, two out of every three Americans make a conscious effort to "buy American." If you count yourself among this group, you face a formidable task.

Determining what is truly American has become increasingly complex in today's global economy. Are those muffins English? Are your fries French? Is that cheese Danish?

Your job as a patriotic consumer is to sort out fact from fiction, a process that can be simplified by focusing on two questions: (a) where is a product manufactured and (b) what is the location of the parent company?

The confusion over "Made in the USA" has been greatly alleviated by government labeling requirements. The origin of imported goods such as Barbie dolls (Malaysia), G.I. Joes (China) and Rawlings' official major league baseballs (Costa Rica) can be easily identified by the product label.

Foreign companies operating in the United States, on the other hand, have become increasingly difficult to detect. Most patriotic consumers are unaware, for example, that many of their most cherished consumer icons—including the Jolly Green Giant, the Pillsbury Dough Boy, and Mr. Bubble—have been bought up by foreign agents.

The signs of foreign infilitration are everywhere. Travel to New York City and look up at the neon advertisements above Times Square (keeping a firm grip on your wallet). Observe the brand names: Sony, Samsung, Suntory, Fuji, TDK, Maxell, Panasonic. Not one is American-owned.

In response to this alarming trend, patriotic consumers across the nation have joined the "Buy American" crusade. Unfortunately, their honest intentions have been exploited by a few crass opportunists—the greedy CEOs and flag waving politicians who pledge allegiance to "Buy American" in public and drive foreign-owned luxury cars in private.

How can a patriotic consumer avoid being manipulated by these false prophets? Education is the key. You must learn to base your purchases on fact rather than instinct. Instinct would tell you, for example, that Grecian Formula is from Greece. It isn't. The same applies to Irish Spring, English Leather, and Dutch Boy paint. Each is all-American.

Conversely, many brand name products you might assume *are* American-owned are not: *TV Guide* (Australia), Burger King (UK), Ex-Lax (Switzerland), Alka-Seltzer (Germany), Good & Plenty (Finland), Tropicana (Canada), Bic shavers (France), and Legos (Denmark).

Thanks to mergers and acquisitions—80 percent of which took place in the past decade—foreign-owned brands in the US marketplace are now at an all-time high; yet, many consumers are unaware of their presence. It is your job as a patriotic consumer to learn, recognize, and identify these products.

Vigilance is required. Every time you go shopping, you must confront a dizzying array of choices: 300 models of cars, 11,000 magazines, and 25,000 items on the supermarket shelves—13,244 new food products were launched in 1990 alone.

Patriotic consumers must make fundamental changes in their buying habits. Above all, they must learn to resist temptation. Foreign-based companies thrive on "impulse buyers," which is a fancy way of saying, people who buy things they don't really need.

Are you willing to give up convenience, lower prices, and better mousetraps for the good of your country? The challenge is yours. The weapons are paper and plastic. Buyer beware.

NOTE: For the purposes of this book, all products are classified according to the location of their parent company, unless otherwise noted. Please be aware that in a global economy ownership changes rapidly. All facts in this book should be weighed accordingly.

Product Ranking	Brand	Country of Ownership
#1 Car	Honda Accord	Japan
#1 Toy company	Nintendo	Japan
#1 Weekly magazine	TV Guide	Australia
#1 Oil producer in US	British Pretroleum	UK
#1 Frozen food entrees	Stouffers	Switzerland
#1 Fax machine	Sharp	Japan
#1 Retail eyewear	Pearle Vision	UK
#1 TV Set	RCA	France
#1 Facial soap	Dove Soap	Netherlands/UK
#1 Premium Ice Cream	Häagen-Dazs	UK
#1 Pop music label	Columbia	Japan
#1 Bottled water	Arrowhead	Switzerland
#1 Hotel chain	Holiday Inn	UK
#1 Consumer electronics	Panasonic	Japan
#1 Laptop computer	Toshiba	Japan
#1 Antacid	Maalox	France
#1 Camera	Canon	Japan
#1 Prepared dough	Pillsbury	UK
#1 Sporting goods	Mizuno	Japan
#1 Bottled water	Arrowhead	Switzerland
#1 Frozen pizza	Totinos	UK
#1 Video camcorder	Sony	Japan
#1 Prescription drug	Amoxil	UK
#1 Sporting goods chain	Herman's	UK

BUY AMERICAN

BUY THIS BOOK

DRINK
AMERICAN
ALCOHOL

Happy hour is over. It's time to sober up, America. Our economy is on the rocks. We've been drinking ourselves into bankruptcy— in 1990, imports of alcohol exceeded exports by $2.7 billion.

Any experienced drinker can tell you the best scotch comes from Scotland, the best gin from England, and the best tequila from Mexico, but America has some alcoholic traditions of its own; for example, sour mash whisky.

Straight from the hills of Kentucky and Tennessee, sour mash whisky is the American spirit—hearty, robust, and powerful enough to knock you off your feet.

Unfortunately, many Americans reach for something lighter at cocktail hour—fruity wines, sweet liqueurs, bubbly champagnes. In other words, drinks for washing down some fancy food at a French restaurant.

Next time, why not belly up to the bar and drink like a real American? Sip a little whisky courtesy of Jim Beam, Jack Daniels, and George Dickel. It's all the proof you'll need.

SUMMARY: Time for some serious drinking. Take a shot of sour mash whisky—no foreign distiller can match it.

ALCOHOL

Liquor (By Country of Manufacture)

■ GIN

Beefeater (England)
Boodles (England)
Bombay (England)
Tanqueray (England)

■ LIQUEUR/
BRANDY/
COGNAC

Amaretto di Saronno (Italy)
Averna (Italy)
Baileys Original Irish Cream (Ireland)
Benedictine (France)
Campari (Italy)
Cointreau (France)
Courvoisier (France)
De Ville (France)
Drambuie (Scotland)
Grand Marnier (France)
Harvey's Bristol Cream (England)
Hennessy (France)
Irish Mist (Ireland)
Jagermeister (German)
Kahlua (Mexico)
Malibu (Canada)
Martell Cognac (Canada)
Metaxa Ouzo (Greece)
Midori (Mexico)
Remy Martin (France)
Sambuca Romana (Italy)
Stock '84 (Italy)

ALCOHOL (Cont.)

■ TEQUILA
Coyote (Mexico)
Jose Cortez (Mexico)
Jose Cuervo
(Mexico)
Juarez (Mexico)
Monte Alban
(Mexico)
Montezuma
(Mexico)
Pepe Lopez (Mexico)
Sauza (Mexico)

■ VERMOUTH
Cinzano (Italy)
Noilly Prat (France)
Santini (Italy)
Stock (Italy)
Tosti (Italy)

■ VODKA
Absolut (Sweden)
Black Death
(Netherlands)
Denaka (Denmark)
Finlandia (Finland)
Icy (Iceland)
Stolyichnaya
(Russia)
Tanqueray (England)
Tarkhuna (Georgia)

■ RUM
Anejo Rum
(Venezuela)
Appleton Rums
(Jamaica)
C.J. Wray (Jamaica)
Cockspur
(Barbados)
Goslings (Bermuda)
Mount Gay
(Barbados)
Myer's Original
(Jamaica)

■ SCOTCH AND
WHISKEY
Ambassador
(Scotland)
Ballantine's
(Scotland)
Bell's (Scotland)
Black & White
(Scotland)
Black Velvet
(Canada)
Bushmills (Ireland)
Calvert Extra
(Canada)
Canadian Club
(Canada)
Canadian Mist
(Canada)
Chivas Regal
(Scotland)
Clan MacGregor
(Scotland)
Crown Royal
(Canada)
Cutty Sark
(Scotland)
Dewar's (Scotland)
Duggan's Dew
(Scotland)
Glenfiddich
(Scotland)
Glenlivet (Scotland)
Highland Park
(Scotland)
Inver House
(Scotland)
Jameson (Ireland)
J&B Scotch
(Scotland)
Johnnie Walker
(Scotland)
Lord Calvert
(Canada)
Macallan (Scotland)
Old Smuggler
(Scotland)
Seagram's VO
(Canada)

The Famous
Grouse
(Scotland)
Vat 69 (Scotland)
White Horse
(Scotland)
Windsor (Canada)

■ BEER AND ALE
Amstel Light
(Netherlands)
Asahi (Japan)
Bass (UK)
Beck's (Germany)
Bohemia (Mexico)
Carlsberg (England)
Carta Blanca
(Mexico)
Corona Extra
(Mexico)
Dos Equis (Mexico)
Foster's (Australia)
Gosser (Austria)
Grolsch
(Netherlands)
Guinness Stout
(Ireland)
Harp (Ireland)
Heineken
(Netherlands)
Holsten (Germany)
John Courage
(England)
Kingfisher (India)
Kirin (Japan)
Kronenbourg
(France)
Labatt's (Canada)
Lowenbrau Zurich
(Switzerland)
Mackeson Triple
Stout (England)
McEwan's
(Scotland)
Molson Ale
(Canada)
Moosehead
(Canada)

ALCOHOL (Cont.)

Negra Modelo
(Mexico)

Newcastle Brown
(England)

O'Keefe's (Canada)

Old Peculiar
(England)

Pilsner Urquell
(Czechoslovakia)

Red Stripe
(Jamaica)

Samuel Smith's
(England)

San Miguel
(Phillipines)

Sapporo (Japan)

Singha (Thailand)

Spaten (Germany)

Steinlager (New
Zealand)

St. Pauli Girl
(Germany)

Suntory (Japan)

Tecate (Mexico)

Tsingtao (China)

Watney's (England)

■ IMPORTED
WINE AND
CHAMPAGNE

(By Country of
Origin)

Asti Spumante
(Italy)

Avia (Yugoslavia)

Blue Nun (Germany)

Bolla (Italy)

Boucheron (France)

Canei (Italy)

Cella (Italy)

Codorniu (France)

Concha Y Toro
(Chile)

Dom Perignon
(France)

Folonari (Italy)

Freixenet (Spain)

Lancer's (Portugal)

Louis Jadot (France)

Goerges Duboef
(France)

Mateus (Portugal)

Möet & Chandon
(France)

Mouton Cadet
(France)

Partager (France)

Piper-Heidsiech
(France)

Principato (Italy)

Reunite (Italy)

Ruffino (Italy)

Tattinger (France)

■ DOMESTIC
WINE AND
CHAMPAGNE

(By Country of
Ownership)

Almaden (UK)

Beaulieu Wines (UK)

Beringer Wines (UK)

Charles Krug
(Canada)

Christian Brothers
(UK)

Domaine Chandon
(UK)

G.H. Mumm & Cie
(Canada)

Inglenook (UK)

Mondavi (Canada)

Monterey Vineyard
(Canada)

Möet-Hennessey
(France)

Mumm Napa Valley
(Canada)

Seagram's Coolers
(Canada)

Sterling Vineyards
(Canada)

DUBIOUS ORIGINS

BUDWEISER BEER

Next time you say Bud, you could be speaking Czech. The American version of Budweiser—which is considered the world's most popular beer—was judged in the 1980s to have infringed on the trademark name of the historic Budweiser Budvar brewery in Ceske Budejouice, Czechoslovakia. As a result, Anheuser Busch is not allowed to sell American Budweiser in heavy beer-drinking countries such as Germany and Austria. In other countries, such as Spain and Italy, the American version is just named Bud. Currently, England is the only country to carry both versions of the beer.

5

ADOPT AMERICAN ANIMALS

Americans love pets. There are an estimated 200 million animals in households nationwide; in fact, according to *American Demographer,* 43 percent of US households have pets, while only 38 percent have children. In recent years, however, the origin of these animals has become increasingly exotic. Instead of a cat named Tabby and a dog named Rover, there is a ferret named Vicious.

Most of these pets are imported. According to the *New York Times,* 30,000 shipments of foreign reptiles, birds, and mammals arrive in the USA each year. Among the most popular are pythons, iguanas, scorpions, tarantulas, and piranhas.

These pets don't come cheap. Thousands of dollars are spent on the rarest species—so rare, in some cases, they're becoming extinct. Why pluck some animal out of its natural habitat, when there are plenty of native American skunks, alligators, and rattlesnakes out in the cold or, worse, lying on the side of the road?

Meanwhile, all over this country, dogs and cats are waiting to be adopted—animals that will give you love and loyalty and won't attack your children unless provoked. Can you say the same about your iguana?

SUMMARY: We've gone from tropical fish and hamsters to scorpions and man-eating pythons. Who are the guinea pigs? American pets.

BUY
AMERICAN
AUTOMOBILES

What went wrong with American cars? Their names, that's what. American cars used to have names that brimmed with confidence. Thunderbird. Mustang. Fifth Avenue. American-sounding names.

Names that made us sound invincible.

Then, sometime in the 1970s, cars with non-American names began appearing. Volare. Torino. Cordoba. And, worst, of all, Pinto. Was it named after a horse or a bean? In terms of combustibility, it was more like the latter.

Like a lot of people in the 70s, the Big Three automakers were trying to seem sophisticated but, just like their cars, the plan backfired. Names like Le Mans and Le Baron paved the road for Le Car from France.

Next, cars went New Age. We got zodiac signs (Taurus), crystals (Prizm), and astrological terms (Saturn, Eclipse). Could Uranus be far behind?

Foreign-sounding cars were arriving by the boatload and nobody seemed to notice. Consumers were confused and they remain that way. The solution? Make American cars *sound* American again.

All you have to do is pick an example of American ingenuity—say, weapons of mass destruction—and start renaming cars after them. The Plymouth Laser becomes the Laser-Guided Missile. The

AUTOMOBILES

■ CARS AND MOTORCYCLES

Acura (Japan)
Alfa Romeo (Italy)
Aston Martin (UK)
Audi (Germany)
Bentley (UK)
BMW (Germany)
Diahatsu (Japan)
Ferrari (Italy)
Honda (Japan)
Hyundai (Korea)
Infiniti (Japan)
Isuzu (Japan)
Kawasaki (Japan)
Lexus (Japan)
Lotus (UK)
Mack Trucks (France)
Maserati (Italy)
Mazda (Japan)
Mercedes-Benz (Germany)
Mitsubishi (Japan)
Nissan (Japan)
Porsche (Germany)
Range Rover (UK)
Rolls Royce (UK)
SAAB (Sweden)
Subaru (Japan)
Suzuki (Japan)
Toyota (Japan)
Volkswagen (Germany)
Volvo (Sweden)
Yugo (Yugoslavia)

■ TIRES

Armstrong (Italy)
Bridgestone (Japan)
Continental (Germany)
Dunlop (Japan)

Dodge Stealth becomes the Stealth Fighter. It's easy.

And after we run out of military hardware, we can start naming cars after American politicians. It worked for the Lincoln Town Car. How about a Ford Rockefeller—doesn't that sound dignified— or maybe a Buick Nixon? The latter might not have a four-year warranty but it *could* have a special car alarm for break-ins.

HOW TO BUY A FOREIGN AMERICAN CAR

Want to buy a sports car? An American sports car? Maybe you've been eyeing an Italian-made Lamborghini Diablo, the fastest factory car in the world, featuring a V-12 engine that tops out at 202.1 MPH.

Well, if you've got the cash, you've got the "Buy America" stamp of approval, because 100 percent of Lamborghini is now owned by Chrysler. Or perhaps you'd prefer a Jaguar, the sleek British roadster. You're in luck—Ford owns 100 percent of Jaguar.

What could be easier? You support the American automobile industry and get a sports car in return. That's a deal few consumers can pass up.

And sports cars are not the only foreign models which have American ownership. Chrysler also has a 15 percent stake in Maserati and 11 percent in Mitsubishi; GM owns 100 percent of Lotus, approximately 50 percent of SAAB and 40 percent of Isuzu; and Ford owns approximately 75 percent of Aston Martin, 24 percent of Mazda and 10 percent of Rover.

Of course, there are trickier ways of owning a foreign-made automobile. You can buy a transplant, i.e., a car made abroad by the Big Three and then shipped to the United States.

The Big Three have made no secret about their use

of foreign labor. General Motors named their Ramos Arizpe plant in Mexico—which assembles Buick Centurys and Chevy Cavaliers—their top plant of the year in 1991.

Ironically, cars assembled south and north of the border are often considered domestic under the Corporate Average Fuel Economy (CAFE) rules administered by the Environmental Protection Agency. Any car with over 75 percent North American content is considered domestic.

It gets confusing. For example, the Honda Accord—the bestselling car in the USA—is built in Marysville, Ohio. For export purposes, the Accord is considered domestic. When purchased in the US, however, it is considered an import.

Currently, over 40 percent of Japanese cars sold in the USA are made in America. Unfortunately, the same statistic does not apply to American cars in Japan. A leading Japanese newspaper recently found that only five out of 1000 Japanese businesspeople surveyed would even consider buying an American car.

And many Americans seem to agree—1,350,000 bought Japanese cars in 1991. Given the woeful state of the American automobile industry, you, too, may have secretly thought about buying a Japanese-manufactured car but worried about the reaction from patriotic friends and neighbors.

Which brings us back to transplants: In 1991, Detroit carmakers imported 164,352 vehicles assembled in Japan to be sold as American cars. In other words, you can now buy an American car made in Japan and feel absolutely no guilt. Of course, the only American thing about one of these babies is the nameplate on its side. But don't worry—your neighbors will never know the difference.

SUMMARY: If you're looking for foreign craftsmanship in an American car, get a transplant.

AUTOS (cont.)

■ MODELS BUILT BY JOINT VENTURE OR BY OTHER AUTOMAKER

Geo Metro (GM-Suzuki)

Geo Metro convertible (Suzuki)

Geo Prizm (GM-Toyota)

Geo Tracker (GM-Suzuki)

Dodge Colt (Mitsubishi)

Dodge Stealth (Mitsubishi)

Eagle Summit (Mitsubishi)

Eagle Talon (Mitsubishi)

Ford Festiva (Kia)

Ford Probe (Mazda)

Isuzu Pickup (Subaru-Isuzu)

Isuzu Rodeo (Subaru-Isuzu)

Mazda Rodeo (Ford)

Mitsubishi Precis (Hyundai)

Plymouth Colt (Mitsubishi)

Plymouth Colt Vista (Mitsubishi)

Plymouth Laser (Mitsubishi)

Pontiac LeMans (Daewoo)

Subaru Legacy (Subaru-Isuzu)

Suzuki Swift (GM-Suzuki)

Toyota Corolla (GM-Toyota)

WHAT IS AN AMERICAN CAR?

Confused about the origin of your car or truck? The following list includes all cars and trucks, model year 1992, which are either assembled abroad or are classified as an import under the CAFE restrictions (see previous page).

Company/model	Country of assembly	Classification
■ ACURA (all)	Japan	Import
■ ALFA ROMEO (all)	Italy	Import
■ ASTON MARTIN (all)	England	Import
■ AUDI (all)	Germany	Import
■ BENTLEY (all)	England	Import
■ BMW (all)	Germany	Import
■ BUICK		
Century**	Mexico	Domestic
Regal	Canada	Domestic
■ CADILLAC		
Allante	USA	Import
■ CHEVROLET		
Geo Metro*	Canada	Domestic
Metro covertible	Japan	Import
Geo Storm	Japan	Import
Lumina	Canada	Domestic
■ DIAHATSU (all)	Japan	Import
■ DODGE		
Colt	Japan	Import
Monaco	Canada	Domestic
Stealth	Japan	Import
■ EAGLE		
Summit 4-door	USA	Import
Summit 3-door, wagon	Japan	Import
Talon	USA	Import
Premier	Canada	Domestic
■ FERRARI (all)	Italy	Import
■ FORD		
Festiva	Korea	Import
Escort	Mexico	Domestic
Tempo	Canada	Domestic
Crown Victoria	Canada	Domestic
■ HONDA		
Civic 3-door*	Canada	Import
Civic 4-door*	USA	Domestic
Civic 4-door*	Japan	Import
CRX	Japan	Import
Accord coupe, wagon*	USA	Domestic
Accord, 4-door*	USA	Domestic
Accord, 4-door*	Japan	Import
Prelude	Japan	Import

Company/model	Country	Classification of assembly
■ HONDA (cont.)		
CRX	Japan	Import
Accord, 4-door*	Japan	Import
Prelude	Japan	Import
■ HYUNDAI		
Excel	Korea	Import
Scoupe	Korea	Import
Elantra	Korea	Import
Sonata	Korea	Import
Sonata	Canada	Import
■ INFINITI (all)	Japan	Import
■ ISUZU (all)	Japan	Import
■ JAGUAR (all)	England	Import
■ LAMBORGHINI (all)	Italy	Import
■ LEXUS (all)	Japan	Import
■ LOTUS (all)	England	Import
■ MASERATI (all)	Italy	Import
■ MAZDA		
323	Japan	Import
Protege	Japan	Import
626**	USA	Import
929	Japan	Import
MX-3	Japan	Import
MX-5	Japan	Import
MX-6*	USA	Import
RX-7	Japan	Import
■ MERCEDES-BENZ (all)	Germany	Import
■ MERCURY		
Tracer	Mexico	Domestic
Topaz	Canada	Domestic
Capri	Australia	Import
Grand Marquis	Canada	Import
■ MITSUBISHI		
Precis	Korea	Import
Mirage 3-door	Japan	Import
Mirage 4-door	USA	Import
Eclipse	USA	Import
Galant	Japan	Import
Expo	Japan	Import
Diamanete	Japan	Import
3000GT	Japan	Import
■ NISSAN		
Sentra	USA	Import
Sentra	Japan	Import
NX 1600/2000	Japan	Import
Stanza	Japan	Import
Maxima	Japan	Import
240SX	Japan	Import
300ZX	Japan	Import
■ OLDSMOBILE (all)	USA	Domestic

Company/model	Country	Classification of assembly
■ PLYMOUTH		
Colt	Japan	Import
Colt Vista	Japan	Import
■ PONTIAC		
LeMans	Korea	Import
■ PORSCHE (all)	Germany	Import
■ ROLLS-ROYCE (all)	England	Import
■ SAAB (all)	Sweden	Import
■ SATURN (all)	USA	Domestic
■ SUBARU		
Justy	Japan	Import
Loyale	Japan	Import
Legacy	Japan	Import
Legacy	USA	Import
SVX	Japan	Import
■ SUZUKI		
Swift*	Canada	Domestic
Swift*	Japan	Import
■ TOYOTA		
Tercel	Japan	Import
Corolla sedans*	USA	Domestic
Corolla sedans*	Japan	Import
Corolla sedans*	Canada	Import
Corolla wagons*	Japan	Import
Pasco	Japan	Import
Camry*	USA	Domestic
Camry*	Japan	Import
Cressida	Japan	Import
Celica	Japan	Import
MR2	Japan	Import
Supra	Japan	Import
■ VOLKSWAGEN		
Fox	Brazil	Import
Golf	Mexico	Import
Jetta	Mexico	Import
Jetta	Germany	Import
Cabriolet	Germany	Import
Passat	Germany	Import
Corrado	Germany	Import
■ VOLVO		
240	Sweden	Import
740 sedans	Sweden	Import
740 wagons	Sweden	Import
740 wagons	Canada	Import
940 sedans	Sweden	Import
940 wagons	Sweden	Import
940 wagons	Canada	Import
960	Sweden	Import

Company/model	Country	Classification of assembly
■ YUGO (all)	Yugoslavia	Import

TRUCKS

■ CHEVROLET		
Vans	Canada	Domestic
Sports van	Canada	Domestic
C/K pickups	Canada	Domestic
C/K extended cab	Canada	Domestic
Geo Tracker*	Canada	Domestic
■ DAIHATSU		
Rocky	Japan	Import
■ DODGE		
Ram vans	Canada	Domestic
Ram vans	Canada	Domestic
Caravan	Canada	Domestic
Regular Caravan C/V	Canada	Domestic
Ram 50	Japan	Import
Ram Club Cab	Mexico	Import
Ramcharger	Mexico	Import
■ FORD		
F-Series pickups	Canada	Domestic
■ GMC		
Vans	Canada	Domestic
Rally wagons	Canada	Domestic
Sierra pickups	Canada	Domestic
Sierra extended cab	Canada	Domestic
W4	Japan	Import
■ ISUZU		
Pickup	USA	Import
Pickup	Japan	Import
Amigo	Japan	Import
Trooper	Japan	Import
Rodeo	USA	Import
■ JEEP		
Wrangler	Canada	Domestic
■ MAZDA		
Pickup	Japan	Import
MPV Japan	Import	
Navajo	USA	Domestic
■ MITSUBISHI (all)	Japan	Import
■ NISSAN		
Pickup	USA	Import
Pickup	Japan	Import
Pathfinder	Japan	Import
■ PLYMOUTH		
Voyager	Canada	Domestic
■ RANGE ROVER (all)	England	Import

FOREIGN CAR INDEX

Company/model	Country	Classification of assembly
■ SUZUKI		
Samurai	Japan	Import
Sidekick*	Canada	Domestic
Sidekick*	Japan	Import
■ TOYOTA		
Pickup	USA	Import
Pickup	Japan	Import
Previa	Japan	Import
4Runner	Japan	Import
Land Cruiser	Japan	Import

Source: *Automotive News*
The designation of import or domestic is based on EPA rules—75% or more US and Canadian content is considered domestic; less than 75% is considered imported. * indicates that the EPA views the combined fleet of such models as imported; ** indicates the EPA treats the combined fleet as domestic. Vehicle names are repeated for models sourced in more than once country.

#1 IN AMERICA

BESTSELLING MOTORCYCLES

#1	Harley-Davidson (USA)
#2	Honda (Japan)
#3	Kawasaki (Japan)
#4	Yamaha (Japan)
#5	Suzuki (Japan)

Source: *New York Times* 4/17/90

MODEL YEAR 1991 CARS AND LIGHT TRUCK SALES

#1	Ford (USA)
#2	Chevrolet/Geo (USA)
#3	Toyota (Japan)
#4	Dodge (USA)
#5	Honda (Japan)
#6	Nissan (Japan)

Source: *Automotive News*

EAT
AMERICAN
CANDY

Do you have a sweet tooth? Did one of your parents have a sweet tooth before you? Are they now wearing dentures? If you answered yes to any of the questions above, you may be a chocoholic.

It sounds harmless enough—until you realize that those little candy bars add up to a massive trade imbalance. Try telling that to a chocoholic. What do you get back? The blank stare of an addict.

Chocoholics are a truly desperate breed. They don't care who the pusher is as long as the supply remains plentiful. Allegiance to one's country means practically nothing to someone who's jonesing for their cocoa/sugar fix.

And that's sad because if chocoholics had a little more self control they might begin to see how foreign companies are feeding their addiction.

There *is* hope. You *can* get that milk chocolate monkey off your back. Next time you're ready to stuff some anonymous candy bar down your throat, pause and reflect for a moment on the state of your country's economy. Remember: the road to recovery is right up the Hershey highway, where there's a Kiss for good luck.

SUMMARY: Chocoholics are tearing the very fabric of America every time they forget their mother's advice: Don't take candy from strangers.

CANDY

After Eight (Switzerland)

Almond Chocolate (Japan)

Alpine White (Switzerland)

Altoids (UK)

Baby Ruth (Switzerland)

Baci Chocolates (Italy)

Beechnut Chewing Gum (UK)

Big Balloon Bubble Gum (Japan)

Bit-O-Honey (Switzerland)

Bon Bon Nuggets (Switzerland)

Butterfinger (Switzerland)

Butternut (Finland)

Callard & Bowser English Toffee (UK)

Chuckles (Finland)

Chunky (Switzerland)

Cote d'Or (Spain)

Dressels (France)

Fanny Farmer (France)

Ferrero Mon Cheri (Italy)

Goobers (Switzerland)

Good 'n Fruity (Finland)

Good & Plenty (Finland)

Heath Bars (Finland)

Jolly Rancher (Finland)

CANDY (cont.)

Lindt Chocolate
(Switzerland)

Lotte (Japan)

Lucky Eggs (Italy)

Malted Milk Eggs
(Finland)

Mentos
(Netherlands)

Milk Duds (Finland)

Milk Shake (Finland)

Nestlés Crunch
(Switzerland)

Nutella (Italy)

Oh Henry!
(Switzerland)

100 Grand
(Switzerland)

Payday (Finland)

Perugina Chocolate
(Italy)

Raisinettes
(Switzerland)

Regal Crown Sour
Candies (UK)

Schrafft's
Chocolates (UK)

Sno Caps
(Switzerland)

Sorrento
(Switzerland)

Switzer Licorice
Bites (Finland)

Tic Tacs (Italy)

Toblerone
(Switzerland)

Twirl Chocolate Bar
(UK)

Werther's Original
(Germany)

Whoppers (Finland)

Willy Wonka Candy
(Switzerland)

Zagnut Bar (Finland)

Zero Bar (Finland)

ICE CREAM

Abbots Old
Philadelphia
(Canada)

Baskin-Robbins (UK)

Choc-O-Malt
(Switzerland)

Colombo Frozen
Yogurt (France)

Creamsicle
(Netherlands/UK)

Dreyer's Grand Ice
Cream
(Bahamas)

Drumstick Sundae
Cone
(Switzerland)

Gold Bond
(Netherlands/
UK)

Good Humor (UK)

Häagen Dazs (UK)

Howard Johnson
(UK)

Louis Sherry
(Canada)

Mister Softee (UK)

Popsicle
(Netherlands/UK)

Push Ups
(Switzerland)

ADVERTISING:
CAVEAT
EMPTOR

Who's selling America? We don't mean literally selling it, as in a large piece of real estate, but selling it to us through advertising. In 1992, the top ten advertising agencies ranked by annual billing included four companies based in England, one in France, and one in Japan.

This is a dangerous trend. Advertisers control the eyes and ears of our nation. There is no escaping it—magazines, newspapers, radio, TV, and billboards all do battle for our attention span and our discretionary income. 61 billion pieces of junk mail are delivered annually by the US Postal Service.

The heartbeat of America is undergoing a stress test and it's no wonder—we're being sound bit to death.

Advertisers continue to spread their false and misleading claims with "lite," "fresh," and "natural" products which aren't anything of the kind. Their slick sloganeering has made cynics of us all. The real thing? Uh-huh?

And now—to make matters worse—we find out that foreigners are the puppeteers pulling the strings on Madison Avenue. Enough is enough. As some great philosopher once said: sometimes you feel like a nut, sometimes you don't.

SUMMARY: Your remote control is in the hands of advertising executives from foreign-owned agencies. Hit the mute button before it hits you.

CELEBRITY:
CAVEAT EMPTOR

After scientists finally figure out the origin of life, their attention should turn to the second most perplexing question in the universe: Why do celebrity endorsements work? Theories abound but the truth is that nobody knows.

All we know is that celebrity sells. The term celebrity, of course, must be used loosely. When it comes to advertising, almost any recognizable face qualifies as a celebrity. Ollie North, G. Gordon Liddy, and Tip O'Neill have all been product spokesmen, for example. And that's just scraping the bottom of the barrel.

Everyone from actor-turned-philanthropist Paul Newman to Orville Redenbacher has their own brand of popcorn. Even fake personalities such as Joe Isuzu and Bartlyes & James have managed to become household names. And you don't have to be alive—Colonel Sanders is still selling Kentucky Fried Chicken long after he kicked the bucket.

Simply put: Americans trust their celebrities. Rarely do they stop to think about the huge sums of money that endorsers are paid or, for that matter, the companies who hire them. It is public knowledge that many of America's biggest stars are cashing checks from abroad, including Michael Jackson (Japan-based Sony Corporation), Whitney Houston (German-owned Arista Records), and Stephen King (UK-based Viking Press).

The number of foreign-owned products endorsed by American celebrities is less well-known, however. Elizabeth Taylor's perfume line, for example, is owned by Unilever (Netherlands/UK). Chances are, her adoring public does not care.

Nor, for that matter, do the kids who blow their allowances on Nintendo (Japan) games endorsed by sports heros such as Bo Jackson, Michael Jordan, Magic Johnson, Larry Bird, Nolan Ryan, Roger Clemens, Jack Nicklaus, John Elway, and Ivan Lendl. Even Mike Tyson has a Nintendo game to help while away the time. Need we say more?

SUMMARY: The cult of personality cuts a wide swath in supermarket aisles. Where's the beef? Celebrity sells but it also sells out.

FOREIGN EMPLOYERS IN THE U.S.

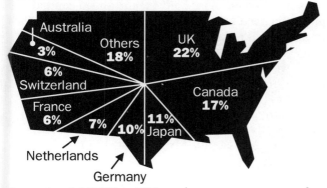

All countries: 4,440,000 in 1990
Source: Bureau of Economic Analysis, *Survey of Current Business,* July 1991

ICONS: CAVEAT EMPTOR

You have to hand it to the British and we do, time and time again, generally in small bills issued by the US treasury. Why do we show our former oppressors such generosity? It's simple: we don't know we're buying British products.

A few—we won't call them devious, we'll just say clever—British conglomerates have realized that the easiest way to an American's wallet is through consumer icons, those beloved childhood companions who used to entertain us into buying their products. Like the Pillsbury Dough Boy.

Well, we hate to break it to you, but the Pillsbury Dough Boy is now making bread for the Brits. He's been bought by a UK-based food conglomerate. So have many popular advertising characters, including the Jolly Green Giant, the Keebler elves, Mister Softee, Mr. Donut, Mr. Bubble, and the Good Humor Man.

Who would suspect the Jolly Green Giant was doing dirty work for the Brits? It's ingenious all right. But keep a stiff upper lip—don't get mad, get even. Next time, we'll play by their rules: an eye for an eye. We'll buy Big Ben so that Uncle Ben can use it to sell his rice. Then we'll see who's laughing. Ho ho ho.

SUMMARY: Many of our favorite consumer icons are modern-day Benedict Arnolds.

DIE
AMERICAN

SKIN CARE

Caress
(Netherlands/UK)
Clarifiance (France)
Clarins (France)
Clean & Smooth
(Germany)
Crabtree and Evelyn
(UK)
Derma-Soft Creme
(Switzerland)
Dove (Netherlands/
UK)
Erno Laszlo
(Netherlands/UK)
Eversoft (Japan)
Jergens (Japan)
Lifebuoy
(Netherlands/UK)
Lever 2000
(Netherlands/UK)
Lux (Netherlands/
UK)
Nivea Facial Cream
(Germany)
Pears (UK)
Plentitude Skin
Care (France)
Ponds Cold Cream
(Netherlands/UK)
Pure & Simple
Lotion (UK)
Renergie (France)
Shield
(Netherlands/UK)
Swisscare (France)
Vaseline Intensive
Care
(Netherlands/UK)
Vital-Perfection
(Japan)
Yardley of London
(Germany)

The American obsession with immortality is scaling new heights. It seems like nobody wants to die anymore. They're too busy taking wonder drugs, getting tummy tucks and aerobicizing on their Stair Master.

We live in a death-defying culture. The signs are everywhere: Movies like *Ghost* and the pseudo-science of cryonics—where people freeze their bodies into the future—point out the desperation of Americans to live forever.

Baby-boomers, in particular, cling to foolish New Age visions of an afterlife, where they can still drive the Volvo station wagon to the discount store for six-packs of bottled water and organic blue corn tortilla chips. Some call it Yuppie heaven; psychologists call it denial.

The age-retarding racket has—not surprisingly—been infiltrated by foreign companies, who know Americans will swallow just about anything that promises a longer life. From the East we get herbs and holistic therapy; from the West we get cosmetic surgery and pharmaceuticals.

These "miracle cures" cost billions of dollars, money that could be spent fixing roads and bridges during our real lifetime. So why not entertain a few unhealthy vices for a change? Live it up! Die American.

SMOKING
GUNS

T hink of Humphrey Bogart as a hardboiled detective or Clint Eastwood as a Western cowboy and what leaps to mind? Cigarettes and guns, that's what. What could be more American?

According to experts, however, both the tobacco and firearm industries are in deep trouble. The former is particularly desperate. What else could account for Marlboro Mediums? Since when has "medium" become an attractive way to market products to American consumers?

The firearms industry, on the other hand, *should* be healthy; after all, there are an estimated 200 million guns in American hands. Still, there is cause for concern: the Colt Manufacturing Company—of Colt .45 six-shooter fame—recently went into Chapter 11.

Once again, imports are to blame. Many law enforcement officials, including the FBI, are turning to foreign brands—the Italian Beretta, the Austrian Glock, and German Sig Sauer—as their weapon of choice.

In 1990 alone, 683,000 handguns were imported into the US with barely a peep from the powerful National Rifle Association. In fact, the NRA *opposed* a ban on importing semiautomatic weapons. How patriotic is that?

SUMMARY: Thinking of "smoking yourself?" Please do it the American way.

TAKE
AMERICAN
DRUGS

E very year the US government pours millions of dollars into the "war on drugs." The DEA confiscates Mexican marijuana, Columbian cocaine, and heroin from Southeast Asia. Meanwhile, boatloads of drugs arrive in this country right under their noses.

What kind of drugs? The drugs that can be found in every home in America—drugs for your stomach, drugs for your skin, drugs for your brain. Little pills, big pills, millions and millions of pills worth billions and billions of dollars.

We're talking prescription and over-the-counter drugs here. OK, sure, they're legal but that doesn't mean we should take them for granted. In fact, large quantities of these drugs are supplied by foreign-owned pharmaceutical companies.

For example, the Swiss—the ones that introduced those addictive chocolate bars into our diets—also make candy for the mind. And like their watches, these drugs don't come cheap.

The Swiss are hardly alone. British-owned firms control a good deal of the $33 billion retail prescription market in the USA. It seems the Brits have a long history of exporting drugs—check out those tales of Victorian opium dens if you don't believe us.

And, of course, we mustn't overlook the Germans. The same company that invented aspirin—Bayer—

DRUGS

■ OVER THE COUNTER MEDICATIONS

Actifed Antihistamine (UK)

Acutrim Appetite Suppressant (Switzerland)

Alka-Seltzer Antacid (Germany)

Bactine Antiseptic (Germany)

Bugs Bunny Vitamins (Germany)

Chocks Vitamins (Germany)

Contac Cold Remedy (UK)

Doan's Pills (Switzerland)

Dulcolax Laxative (Germany)

Ecotrin Analgesic (UK)

Ex-Lax Laxative (Switzerland)

Fletcher's Castoria Laxative (Japan)

Flintstones Vitamins (Germany)

Gas-X Antacid (Switzerland)

Geritol Vitamin Supplement (UK)

Habitrol Nicotine System (Switzerland)

Kellogg's Castor Oil (UK)

Maalox Antacid (France)

Medi-Quick First-Aid Ointment (Japan)

also sent out free samples of heroin to the German public at the turn of the century. That's one way of hooking a customer.

SUMMARY: Just say no to the Swiss, British, and German drug cartels. Buy American drugs.

TOP FIVE PRESCRIPTION PRODUCTS DISPENSED

#1	Amoxil (UK)
#2	Lanoxin (UK)
#3	Zantac (Switzerland)
#4	Premarin (USA)
#5	Xanax (USA)

Source: *Drug Store News*, June 1991.

ANTACIDS

#1	Maalox (France)
#2	Mylanta (USA)
#3	Tums (UK)
#4	Rolaids (USA)
#5	Alka-Seltzer (Germany)

Source: *Adweek's Marketing Week*, Superbrands, 1991

STOLICHNAYA VODKA

Question: What does Pepsico receive from the Russians in exchange for the right to sell and distribute Pepsi? Answer: Stolichnaya vodka. They get it straight up—literally—thanks to an 1972 agreement that allowed Pepsi to become the first consumer product to be sold in the then-Soviet Union in exchange for cases of Stolichnaya, the world-famous vodka. Although their name sounds foreign, Monsieur Henri Wines, Stoly's distributer in the US, is a division of Pepsico of Purchase, New York. Does this mean that drinking Stolichnaya is drinking American? We think nyet.

BUY AMERICAN ELECTRONICS

■ CONSUMER ELECTRONICS: COMPUTERS

Aiwa (Japan)
Akai (Japan)
Bang and Olufsen (Denmark)
Brother (Japan)
Canon (Japan)
Casio (Japan)
Clarion (Japan)
Daewood (Korea)
Denon (Japan)
Epson (Japan)
Fujitsu (Japan)
General Electric (France)
Goldstar (Korean)
Hitachi (Japan)
Honeywell (France)
JVC (Japan)
Kenwood (Japan)
Leading Edge (Japan)
Magnavox (Netherlands)
Mita (Japan)
Mitsubishi (Japan)
Murata (Japan)
Nakamichi (Japan)
National (Japan)
NEC (Japan)
Oki (Japan)
Okidata (Japan)
Olivetti (Italy)
Onkyo (Japan)
Panasonic (Japan)
Phillips (Netherlands)
Philco (Netherlands)
Pioneer (Japan)

Japanese electronic companies have pulled off one the greatest tactical manuevers in the history of capitalism. First, they sold us billions of dollars worth of machines to watch and listen to American entertainment. Then they bought the entertainment.

What did Americans get in return? Compact discs to replace our old, still-playable records and VCRs to watch movies that were playing at our neighborhood theaters, that's what. In other words, not much. And to add insult to injury, most of the technology was developed in the USA.

Many Americans were shocked and angered when these electronics companies used the money they made from American consumers to buy up American movie studios and record labels. However, there must still be a few more entertainment companies for sale because—believe it or not—even more electronic formats are on the way, including DAT (digital audio tape), MD (mini disk), DCC (digital compact), DBS (direct broadcast satellite) and the big kahuna—HDTV (high definition television).

Future technology will be geared towards consumers who prefer to stay within the safe confines of their home. For example, the FCC has just given out first licenses to Interactive Video Data Service (IVDS) networks, which will allow consumers to make transactions—like ordering a pizza—through their television sets.

ELECTRONICS (cont.)

RCA (France)
Ricoh (Japan)
Quasar (Japan)
Samsung (Korean)
Sansui (Japan)
Sanyo Fisher
(Japan)
Sharp (Japan)
Siemens (Germany)
Seiko (Japan)
Sylvania
(Netherlands)
Smith Corona (UK)
Sony (Japan)
TDK (Japan)
TEAC (Japan)
Technics (Japan)
Toshiba (Japan)
Victor (Japan)
Philips
(Netherlands)
Zenith Data System
(France)

■ HOME
APPLIANCES

A.B. Dick (UK)
Anchor Brush
(Netherlands)
Bridgestone
batteries (Japan)
Eureka vacuums
(Sweden)
Farberware (UK)
Fridgidaire (Sweden)
Genie(Netherlands)
Gibson stoves
(Sweden)
Halsey Taylor
Drinking
Fountains (UK)
Jacuzzi (UK)
JetVac
(Netherlands)

We are wired-up for a telecommunications revolution. Fiber optics and satellites have already bridged the continental divide. But is sitting in bumper-to-bumper traffic with your car phone, on-hold, really a sign of evolution? Have fax and telephone answering machines made your life more convenient or less?

Before you rush off and buy one of these high-tech formats, remember that not too long ago, 8-track tapes were considered the hot technology. Today, you can't even give 8-tracks away at your garage sale. The same goes for Betamax.

So don't forget that great American saying next time you're browsing through an electronic store: Once a fool, twice a sucker.

SUMMARY: Expensive new electronic formats for home entertainment are on the way. Will you be buying? Foreign companies are banking on it.

P.S. Keep an eye on the Dutch.

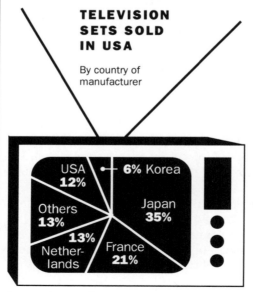

TELEVISION SETS SOLD IN USA

By country of manufacturer

USA 12%
6% Korea
Others 13%
Japan 35%
13% Netherlands
France 21%

Source: *Appliance Magazine,* 1990

ELECTRONICS (cont.)

Kelvinator (Sweden)

Krups (France)

Norelco (Netherlands)

Noritake Dinnerware (Japan)

NuTone (UK)

Philips Light Bulbs (Netherlands)

Royal Doulton Fine China (UK)

Schick Electric Razors (Netherlands)

Singer Sewing Machines (Hong Kong)

Sinkmaster (Sweden)

Swiss Army Knife (Switzerland)

Tappan (Sweden)

Thermos (Japan)

Toledo Scales (Switzerland)

Viking Sewing Machines (Sweden)

Villeroy and Boch Tableware (Germany)

Waterford Glass (UK)

Whirlaway (Sweden)

■ CAMERAS

AEG Olympia (Germany)

Agfa Photography (Germany)

Canon (Japan)

Fujica (Japan)

Hasselblad (Germany)

Konica (Japan)

Leica (Switzerland)

Minolta (Japan)

Olympus (Japan)

Nikon (Japan)

Pentax (Japan)

Ricoh (Japan)

■ FILM AND TAPE

BASF (Germany)

Denon (Japan)

Fuji (Japan)

Maxell (Japan)

Memorex (Netherlands)

TDK (Japan)

Vivatir (Australia)

■ CLOCKS AND WATCHES

Armitron (Japan)

Audemars (Switzerland)

Breitling (Switzerland)

Bulgari (Italy)

Casio (Japan)

Cellini (Switzerland)

Chanel (France)

Citizen (Japan)

Edel (Switzerland)

ETA (Switzerland)

Flik-Flak (Switzerland)

Fouineteau (France)

F.W. Elliot (UK)

Jaeger Le Coultre (Switzerland)

Haller Clock (Germany)

Hamilton (Switzerland)

Heinz Jauch (Germany)

Heuer (Switzerland)

Helix (UK)

Longines (Switzerland)

Omega (Switzerland)

Patek (Switzerland)

Piaget (Switzerland)

Pulsar (Japan)

Rado (Switzerland)

Rolex (Switzerland)

Seiko (Japan)

Spartus (UK)

Swatch (Switzerland)

Tourneau (Switzerland)

■ WRITING INSTRUMENT

Bic (France)

Helix (UK)

Fouineteau (France)

KOH-I-NOOR (Germany)

Letraset (Sweden)

Mont Blanc (Germany)

Parker (UK)

Pentel (Japan)

Pilot (Japan)

Sheaffer (Switzerland)

Staedtler (Germany)

27

BUYING ELVIS

Patriotic consumers in search of a role model need look no further than Elvis Presley, the George Washington of buying American. The King of Rock'n'Roll was a legendary consumer who gave away Cadillacs and shot up TV sets faster than he could buy them.

For a seminar in "buying Elvis," visit Graceland in Memphis, Tennessee. Stop and admire the King's fleet of Cadillacs and—for a few extra buckeroos—tour the inside of his all-American 727. Who else but Elvis would fly his plane to Denver for a peanut butter and jelly sandwich?

Elvis was larger than life and now he's even bigger than death thanks to the 29¢ Elvis stamp. Up in rock'n'roll heaven, Elvis is beaming with pride, knowing how the stamp in his honor is helping to reduce the national debt.

Elvis loved his country and it loved him back. He showed his gratitude by never performing abroad; in fact, the only time Elvis ever left the United States was to serve Uncle Sam. Despite having his hair shaved off, Elvis served his country with pride. Many years later he would be deputized by the Federal Narcotics Bureau. . .but that's another story.

SUMMARY: Elvis may have left the building of life but his spirit lives on through the Elvis stamp. Help your country—buy Elvis and buy often.

WEAR
AMERICAN
FASHION

T he world of high fashion used to be reserved for Hollywood celebrities and other pillars of society. In other words, the people who could afford it. Then, in the 1970's, designer jeans came along and changed everything. Suddenly, all sorts of normal clothes sprouted designer labels, usually with strange, hard-to-pronounce names like Giorgio and Yves.

Of course, the very idea that you could improve on Levi's was, at heart, a perversion of American ideals. Blue jeans are the epitome of democratic fashion: both sexes can wear them, anyone can afford a pair, and, best of all, they improve with age. In Japan, where they seem to understand the value of American fashion, a pair of 1950s Levi's can fetch up to $2000.

Designer fashion is completely at odds with the rugged individualism that made this country great. Look at your history. The pioneers didn't "dress for success" as they conquered the West. In those days, the only fashion accessory was a bootstrap.

Modern fashion designers prey upon the chic (and their wannabes), but, in the end, they're just peddling an expensive form of conformity. So, remember, vogue and glamour are in your mind, not in a magazine.

SUMMARY: American fashion can be summed up in one word: Levi's. Don't settle for less—you'll only pay more.

OUACHITA TECHNICAL COLLEGE

FASHION (cont.)

Revillon (France)

Rive Gauche (France)

Yves St. Laurent (France)

■ SHOES & ACCESORIES

Bally of Switzerland (Switzerland)

Dr. Maartens (UK)

Chaus (UK)

Christian Dior (Italy)

Durango Boots (UK)

Endicott Johnson (UK)

Etienne Aigner (UK)

Frye Boots (UK)

Georgia Boots (UK)

Gucci (Italy)

Michael Stevens (UK)

Vittorio Ricci (Italy)

■ HAIR CARE

Aqua Net Hairspray (Netherlands/UK)

Brylcreem (UK)

Colorative Hair Care (France)

Design Hair Care (Germany)

Falcon Men's Hairspray (UK)

Free & Lovely Antidandruff Foam (UK)

Just Wonderful (Netherlands/UK)

L'Oreal Hair (France)

Neet Hair Remover (UK)

Rave Hair Products (Netherlands/UK)

So Fine Hair Conditioner (Germany)

Wella Balsam (Germany)

■ DENTAL CARE

Aim Toothpaste (Netherlands/UK)

Aqua-Fresh Toothpaste (UK)

Butler Dental Floss (Japan)

Close-Up Toothpaste (Netherlands/UK)

G-U-M Toothbrush (Japan)

Maclean Toothpaste (UK)

Orafix Denture Adhesives (UK)

Pepsodent Toothpaste (Netherlands/UK)

Rinse Mouthwash (Netherlands/UK)

Signal Mouthwash (Netherlands)

EAT
AMERICAN
FOOD

Y ou know the taste of America is changing when ketchup is no longer the country's favorite condiment. It's been replaced by salsa, which neither tastes nor sounds remotely American.

No cause for alarm? Perhaps you'd be interested to know that certain major league baseball stadiums are now selling sushi at their concession stands. Even hallowed Yankee Stadium briefly offered raw clams. What's wrong with a good old fashioned American hot dog, you ask?

Well, aside from the insect parts, just how American *are* hot dogs? Some food purists would argue they're just a cheap imitation of German frankfurters.

The question of food origins grows more confusing all the time. We feel confident that chili doesn't come from Chile, or turkey from Turkey, but what about kiwis and muesli? Where did they come from and, more importantly, why?

Every day another gastronomic tradition is turned upside down. Even our fresh produce sounds suspicious. Are those sprouts really from Brussels? Is that endive Belgian? Good luck finding out.

Check your menu for steak and potatoes and what do you find? Greek salads and Spanish omelettes. Open your refrigerator door and what do you see? Ramen noodles, bean curd, and yogurt. Is it any

FOOD

- FOOD
Adolph's Meat
    Tenderizer
    (Netherlands/UK)
All Ready Pie
    Crusts (UK)
Aunt Nellie's Farm
    Kitchens(UK)
Bernardi Italian
    Foods (UK)
Bertolli Olive Oil
    (Italy)
Bumble Bee Tuna
    (Thailand)
Carnation
    Evaporated Milk
    (Switzerland)
Carr's Table Water
    Crackers (UK)
Cattleman's
    Bar-B-Q (UK)
Chef Francisco
    (Canada)
Chicken Tonight
    (Netherlands/UK)
Club Crackers (UK)
Coffee-Mate
    Non-dairy
    Creamer
    (Switzerland)
Connoisseur Tuna
    Fish (Canada)
Contadina Fresh
    Pasta
    (Switzerland)
Country Crock
    (Netherlands/UK)
Crosse & Blackwell
    (Switzerland)
Cup-A-Soup
    (Netherlands/UK)
Cup O'Noodles
    (Japan)
DAK ham (Denmark)

wonder the Heimlich maneuver was invented by a foreigner?

Out of desperation, diners are taking refuge in generic fast food restaurants, where the menu never changes and neither does the taste. Little do they realize how many of these franchises are owned by foreigners, including Burger King (UK), Dunkin' Donuts (UK), and Hardees (Canada).

So what's a hungry patriot to do? Well, there *is* one sure way to eat American—just follow the signs to Mom's. It's not listed in the Yellow Pages but every town has one—it could be the local diner, or a sandwich shop, it may even be called Dad's, but it tastes and feels like home.

Mom's serves only American food. Two eggs over easy with a side of grits. Cheeseburger and onion rings. A short stack of pancakes. Chipped beef on toast. And if you're real nice, the waitress might even call you "honey."

SUMMARY: Bye bye, Miss American pie. Say hello to salsa and sushi.

FROZEN PIZZA SALES IN THE USA

Source: *Star Tribune* March 19, 1990.

FOOD (cont.)

Lea & Perrins
Worchester
Sauce (France)

Lean Cuisine
(Switzerland)

Lesueur Peas (UK)

Libby's Fruit Juices
(Switzerland)

Lipton's Soup
(Netherlands/UK)

Marinade in
Minutes
(Netherlands/UK)

Mermaid Table Salt
(UK)

Mitchell's Apple
Sauce (UK)

Modern Maid Mixes
(UK)

Mom's Margarine
(Netherlands/UK)

Mott's Apple Sauce
(UK)

Mrs. Butterworth
(Netherlands/UK)

Mrs. Filbert's
Margarine
(Netherlands/UK)

Mr. & Mrs. T
Cocktail Mix (UK)

Munch 'ems (UK)

Oodles Of Noodles
(Japan)

Oregon Farms
(Canada)

Pam Non-Stick
Cooking
Spray(UK)

Peter Pan Seafoods
(Japan)

Pillsbury Dough (UK)

Pizzarias (UK)

Promise Margarine
(Netherlands/UK)

Ragú Sauces
(Netherlands/UK)

Samyang Cup
Ramen (South
Korea)

Sharwood's Spices
(UK)

Shedd's Country
Crock (UK)

Sorrento Cheese
(France)

Spice Islands
Spices (Australia)

Star Brand Olive Oil
(Spain)

Stoned Wheat
Thins (Canada)

Stouffer Frozen
Food
(Switzerland)

Stroehmann
Sunbeam Baked
Goods (Canada)

Sunkist Fun Fruit
Snacks
(Netherlands/UK)

Tio Sancho
Mexican
(Netherlands/UK)

Toll House
(Switzerland)

Totino's Pizza (UK)

Town House
Crackers (UK)

Van de Kamp's
Frozen Foods
(UK)

Wasa Crispbread
(Switzerland)

Weetabix Cereal
(UK)

Wish-Bone Salad
Dressing
(Netherlands/UK)

Yogplait Yogurt
(France)

■ FAST FOOD
FRANCHISES

Baskin-Robbins (UK)

Benihana (Japan)

Burger King (UK)

Carvel (Bahrain)

Dunkin' Donuts (UK)

Fanny Farmer
Candy Shops
(France)

Hardees (Canada)

Häagen-Dazs (UK)

Mister Donut (UK)

Mister Softee (UK)

Roy Rogers
(Canada)

Rusty Scupper
(Switzerland)

Stouffer
(Switzerland)

Winchell's Donut
House (Canada)

■ BEVERAGES

Canada Dry (UK)

Carnation Hot
Cocoa
(Switzerland)

Clamato (UK)

Hires (UK)

Horlick's Malted
Milk (UK)

Kern's Fruit Juices
(Switzerland)

Mott's Apple Juice
(UK)

Ocean Spray (UK)

Orangina (France)

Orange Crush (UK)

Ovaltine
(Switzerland)

Nestles Quik
(Switzerland)

Red Cheek Apple
Juice (UK)

Rose's Lime Juice
(UK)

Schweppes (UK)

Soho Natural
Sodas (Canada)

Sunkist Soda (UK)

Schweppes (UK)

10-K (Japan)

FOOD (cont.)

Tropicana (Canada)

Tree Top Fruit
   Drinks
   (Netherlands/UK)

Wyler's Lemonade
   (UK)

Yoo Hoo (France)

■ COFFEE AND TEA

Bustelo (UK)

Cain's (Switzerland)

Chase and Sanborn
   (Switzerland)

El Pico (UK)

Hills Brothers
   (Switzerland)

El Pico (UK)

Lipton
   (Netherlands/UK)

Medaglia d'Or (UK)

MJB (Switzerland)

Nescafe
   (Switzerland)

Nestea (Switzerland)

Savarin Coffee (UK)

Sunrise
   (Switzerland)

Taster's Choice
   (Switzerland)

Tetley's (UK)

Twinings (UK)

DUBIOUS ORIGINS

FLORIDA ORANGE JUICE

Just because your fresh-tasting glass of orange juice has Florida's Seal of Approval does not mean that it comes from the United States. In 1991, 320,000,000 gallons-worth of frozen citrus concentrate were shipped to the United States from Brazil and then reconstituted, packaged, and sold to American consumers. Under the guidelines of the Florida Department of Citrus, any orange juice, regardless of origin, can receive the Florida Seal of Approval provided it meets state standards. Only the "100% Florida" label guarantees an American-grown glass of orange juice.

INVEST
AMERICAN

INVEST AMERICAN: TRASH

Landfills around the country are overflowing. American cities and corporations are desperately searching for places to dump their waste. Why not offer them your own backyard?

Think of the benefits of living next to a landfill. No more griping about whose turn it is to take out the trash—just chuck it out the back door. Don't worry about the neighbors. When those hefty "host fees" begin rolling into municipal coffers, everybody's property taxes will go down.

The future of American garbage is limitless. Take a look at Wayne Huizenga, the proud new owner of the Florida Marlins expansion baseball franchise. Huizenga made his fortune picking up and disposing of garbage. His trash hauling firm, Waste Management Inc., netted him a cool $13 million. He used that money to start Blockbuster Video, and later bought 15 percent of the Miami Dolphins and a chunk of Joe Robbie Stadium. A real American success story.

So next time you see a litterbug dumping garbage in your neighborhood, don't curse. Remember: that's not trash, that's an investment.

INVESTMENT STRATEGY: There's gold in them there trash hills. Scoop it up before seagulls, rats, and foreign investors get to it first.

INVEST AMERICAN: JAILS

Crime doesn't pay? Know any other jokes? Crime pays better than McDonalds, my friend. According to the Rand Corporation, professional burglars commit between 76 and 118 burglaries a year, while shoplifters and pickpockets average between 135 and 202 thefts.

The real question, of course, is not whether crime pays but how you can make it pay for you. One legal way into the racket is to invest in jail cells. Private penitentaries are a solid financial investment; in fact, several are already turning a profit.

Think of it this way: the US has never had a shortage of criminals. No matter how many you jail, there will always be more serial killers, embezzling televangelists, Uzi-wielding postal employees, celebrity rapists, sleazy insider traders, drug cartel kingpins, computer virus makers, and other assorted forms of human refuse.

In short, the penitentiary industry has explosive growth potential. Look at state money budgeted for the justice system—over half of it is for jails. Figure they spend about $50,000 per cell. That's a lot of loot. There are over 750,000 Americans in jail and plenty more on the way. So get in while it's hot.

INVESTMENT STRATEGY: Do not stop, go directly to jails.

INVEST AMERICAN: 90s NOSTALGIA

The early 90s have not exactly been a party so far—from silicon chips to silicone implants our country is sagging. Some pundits, in fact, have already written this decade off.

As usual, they're dead wrong. Remember what they said about the 70s? No one in their right mind thought artifacts from the era of *Saturday Night Fever,* like disco platform shoes, would come back into style—but they did, proving, once again, that one guy's Watergate is another guy's Wonder Years.

The cultural junkyard is littered with all sorts of fads from the past. First there was the 50s revival of *Happy Days* and *Grease.* Suddenly, old bowling shirts were worth big money. Then came the 60s revival and its psychedelic accessories—fringe jackets, peace signs, and lava lamps.

Now, everbody's having a garage sale. The problem with nostalgia, however, is that no new jobs are created. The solution? Celebrate nostalgia *now.*

In other words, go out and buy everything you can from *Beverly Hills 90210, The Simpsons,* and any other pop culture phenomenon that comes along. You'll stimulate the economy, create jobs, and— trust us—one day you'll be able to put your grandchildren through college.

If everyone cooperates, we'll be able to bring back the 90s *today.*

INVESTMENT STRATEGY: Buy 90s nostalgia items while they're still affordable.

INVEST AMERICAN: BUY 'EM BACK

Many patriotic consumers are still reeling from the shock of their favorite American companies being bought out by foreign investors. Well, it's time to stop seething and do something. Let's buy 'em back!

Over 800 foreign-owned companies in 38 companies are traded on the U.S. stock exchange. What are you waiting for? Pick your favorite company, call your stock broker, get an office pool going, collect door to door—whatever it takes.

Buy back Holiday Inn! Buy back Dunkin' Donuts! Buy back Burger King! Buy back the Pillsbury Dough Boy! Buy back the Jolly Green Giant! Buy back Mr. Bubble! Buy back Universal Studios! Buy back Pebble Beach! Buy back RCA Records (do it for Elvis)! Buy back *TV Guide!* Buy back the Good Humor Man! Buy back Rockefeller Center! Buy back Columbia Pictures!

Sure, maybe we can't buy back every single company, but we *can* try. If everybody pitched in ten bucks every time some foreign investor made an offer for an American company, there would be no more hostile takeovers.

So buy back Radio City Music Hall and make sure you get the Rockettes in the deal. If they don't let you have them, buy back Smith & Wesson!

INVESTMENT STRATEGY: Buy 'em back! Use credit cards if necessary.

TOILETS

Recent Japanese imports in the American toilet industry are giving "dumping products" an entirely new meaning. High-tech commodes from Japan—which retail for as much as $12,000—include a variety of new features such as micro-processor-controlled toilet seats, warm water spray nozzles, built-in dryers, and recorded music. The US industry leaders—American Standard and Kohler Co.—are taking the Japanese toilet challenge seriously. In 1989, Toto Ltd., Japan's leading maker of bathroom fixtures, became the first company to take a crack at the US marketplace with its Washlet unit. Its top model, the Washlet Queen, can analyze urine, measure blood pressure, and send the test results to a physician.

NOT MADE IN AMERICA

I t's perfectly acceptable that some products are manufactured abroad—like those little umbrellas used for tropical drinks, for example. But we draw the line at Americana. If you have to be born in America to become President, it seems only fair that the same standard should apply to other national symbols.

Sadly, many of our country's most beloved icons are no longer made in America. Raggedy Ann dolls are manufactured in China, the Cadillac Allante's body comes from Italy and official NBA basketballs are made in South Korea. Even *The Simpsons* is animated abroad!

It all started with the Statue of Liberty. We're not talking about the Statue itself (which *was* made in France); we're talking about those cheap Lady Liberty pencil sharpeners from Taiwan.

Don't tell us that a country which sent the first man to the moon can't make a lousy souvenir? Well, of course we can make a lousy souvenir—that's not the point.

The point is the American standard used to be more than a toilet. Let's keep it that way.

SUMMARY: Buy American *by Americans* when you buy American.

THE TOWN CALLED USA

Before World War II, products stamped MADE IN USA were not necessarily made in the United States or its territories. Many items, for instance, were made in the town of Usa, Japan (current pop: 27,994). Usa is known to most tourists as the homeplace to a rare and beautiful Shinto shrine to the martial god Hachiman. However, prior to World War II the town was notorious for its manufacture of articles stamped MADE IN USA, which, according to the Encyclopedia Americana, was used "as a means of circumventing American boycotts of Japanese goods," Incidentally, there are two other countries with towns named Usa—Russia and Tanzania.

AMERICAN QUILTS

In 1992, the Smithsonian Institute outraged American quilt makers by licensing the reproduction of four antique quilts in its collection to a firm in China. The American quilt industry protested that the Smithsonian had undercut their business and cheapened the quality of traditional quilting. The Chinese replicas, which can be mass-produced at a fraction of the cost due to cheap labor, were available for $200-400 at the Smithsonian gift shop as well as through the Land's End and Speigel catalogs. Only a removable hang tag identified the quilts as imports. Ironically, one of the quilt patterns was "America's Great Seal."

AMERICAN FLAGS

According to industry experts, approximately 15 percent of all American flags are imported from abroad. This phenomenon is not new: prior to World War II, the American Legion of Cambria County, PA, complained it was "unable to find any small American flags that were not made in either Germany or Japan." In recent times, Taiwan has become the primary source of imported flags, although these imports are often difficult to detect due to tear-off labels. The easiest way to spot an imported flag, experts say, is by its quality—printed rather than stitched—and colors, which rarely match the official Old Glory red, Old Glory white, and Old Glory blue.

WATCH
AMERICAN
MOVIES

Giving an Academy Award for Best Foreign Film is like buying the Ayatollah a tank of gas—nice gesture, but not exactly necessary. Just about every Hollywood movie is made by foreigners anyway.

What we *really* need is an award for Best All-American Film. Let's start with actors. Ever since Vivien Leigh played Scarlett O'Hara in *Gone With The Wind,* British actors have been walking away with *our* Oscars. Nowadays, foreign accents come in all flavors, and every little kid can do impressions of our biggest action-movie stars—Arnold Schwarzenegger (Austria) and Claude van Damme (Belgium). These guys are winning where it counts—at the box office.

And who is running that box office, you ask? One of the biggest movie theater chains in America, Cineplex Odeon, is Canadian-owned. Feel cheated? Misled? That's nothing—scores of movies are being shot north of the border right now, with Canadian cities masquerading as American ones.

And who is shooting these movies, you ask? Foreign directors working for foreign companies, that's who. Several Hollywood studios, including Columbia and Universal, are now owned by Japanese companies; an Australian immigrant owns 20th Century Fox; and a French bank owns MGM.

SUMMARY: Giving foreigners their own Academy Award is not only redundant, it probably just encourages them.

MOTION PICTURE ACADEMY AWARDS

YEAR	BEST ACTOR	BIRTHPLACE
1991	Anthony Hopkins	(England)
1990	Jeremy Irons	(England)
1989	Daniel Day Lewis	(England)
1982	Ben Kingsley	(England)
1976	Peter Finch	(England)
1964	Rex Harrison	(England)
1961	Maximilian Schell	(Austria)
1958	David Niven	(England)
1957	Alec Guinness	(England)
1956	Yule Brynner	(Japan)
1950	Jose Ferrer	(Puerto Rico)
1948	Laurence Olivier	(England)
1947	Ronald Colman	(England)
1943	Paul Lukas	(Hungary)
1939	Robert Donat	(England)
1935	Victor McLaglen	(England)
1932-33	Charles Laughton	(England)
1929-30	George Arliss	(England)

YEAR	BEST ACTRESS	BIRTHPLACE
1990	Jessica Tandy	(England)
1973	Glenda Jackson	(England)
1970	Glenda Jackson	(England)
1969	Maggie Smith	(England)
1965	Julie Christie	(India)
1964	Julie Andrews	(England)
1961	Sophia Loren	(Italy)
1959	Simone Signoret	(Germany)
1956	Ingrid Bergman	(Sweden)
1953	Audrey Hepburn	(Belgium)
1951	Vivien Leigh	(England)
1949	Olivia de Havilland	(Japan)
1946	Olivia de Havilland	(Japan)
1944	Ingrid Bergman	(Sweden)
1942	Greer Garson	(England)
1941	Joan Fontaine	(Japan)
1939	Vivien Leigh	(England)
1937	Luise Rainer	(England)
1936	Luise Rainer	(England)
1934	Claudette Colbert	(France)
1930-31	Marie Dressler	(Canada)

LISTEN
TO AMERICAN
MUSIC

MUSIC

■ RECORD LABELS

A&M (Netherlands)

Arista (Germany)

Capitol Records
(UK)

Casablanca
(Netherlands)

CBS Records
(Japan)

Chess (Japan)

Chryalis (Japan)

Columbia (Japan)

Decca (Netherlands)

Delicious Vinyl
(Netherlands)

Deutsche
Grammophon
(Netherlands)

EMI (UK)

Epic (Japan)

Factory (UK)

Fontana
(Netherlands)

4th and Broadway
(Netherlands)

Geffen (Japan)

IRS (Netherlands)

Island (Netherlands)

Liberty (UK)

London
(Netherlands)

Mango
(Netherlands)

Manhattan (UK)

Mercury
(Netherlands)

MCA (Japan)

Morgan Creek
(Netherlands)

Philips
(Netherlands)

Polydor
(Netherlands)

People all over the world are listening to American music—rock, soul, country and western, jazz, and blues. In England, they listen particularly closely, and for good reason: they're looking for the next musical trend to rip off and sell back to the gullible American record-buying public.

The constant influx of English pop hits on the American charts is one of the devious ways the UK manages to level their trade imbalance (it's certainly not their cuisine).

The "British Invasion" began in 1964 when the Beatles arrived at JFK airport and it hasn't let up since. The tactics *have* changed, however. Today's British performers have perfected their counterfeit craft by disguising their accents and singing 'American.'

It takes a vigilant and keen-eyed consumer to spot these imposters. The first step is to learn to recognize the telltale signs; for example, the combination of good haircuts and bad teeth is a dead giveaway. So are names such as Nigel, Elton, Ian, Sid, and Ringo.

Look out—they're even beginning to rap.

SUMMARY: Ever since Francis Scott Key stole the melody of *The Star-Spangled Banner* from a popular English drinking song, the British have been exacting their revenge on our hit parade. Accept no substitute—buy American music.

MUSIC (cont.)

Polygram
(Netherlands)

RCA (Germany)

SBK (UK)

Smash(Netherlands)

Tuff Gong
(Netherlands)

Uptown (Japan)

Verve (Netherlands)

Virgin (UK)

■ MUSICAL
INSTRUMENTS

Casio (Japan)

Hohner (Germany)

Kawai (Japan)

Roland (Japan)

Yamaha (Japan)

TOP COUNTRY MUSIC LABELS, 1991

#1	MCA (Japan)
#2	RCA (Germany)
#3	Columbia (Japan)
#4	Capitol (UK)
#5	Warner Brothers (USA)

Source: *Billboard,* December 21, 1991

BRITISH BAND NAMES

British musicians have borrowed American musical styles
and American names. The Beatles started the trend by naming themselves after the Crickets, the band of American
rocker Buddy Holly. The Rolling Stones soon followed with an
homage to Mississippi bluesman Muddy Waters and his
song *Rolling Stone.* Then, the Yardbirds named themselves
after jazz great Charlie Parker; Pink Floyd after two bluesmen
from Georgia, Pink Anderson and Floyd Council; and, another
60s band, the Searchers, took their name from a John
Wayne movie. In the 70s, Elvis Costello (real name Declan
Mac Manus) took the King's name in vain. More recent examples include the Dylans and a British band calling itself
Texas.

SHOP
AMERICAN

No doubt about it—America loves its malls. We have mini-malls and mega-malls sprawling all over this great land. But did you ever wonder who's running the store?

Back in the days of Mom and Pop shops, the answer was staring at you from behind the cash register. It may seem corny now, but there was a certain familiarity, not to mention intimacy, about your corner store. Then came the malls. Bye bye, Mom and Pop.

Now we don't know who owns what. In fact, most shoppers are unaware how many prestigious stores—including Saks Fifth Avenue (Bahrain), Bloomingdale's (Canada) and Brooks Brothers (UK)—were bought by foreign investors in the merger mania of the 1980s.

By no means is foreign ownership limited, however, to high-class department stores; supermarkets like A&P (Germany) and sporting goods stores such as Herman's Sporting World (UK) are also owned abroad.

Get the picture? Did you get it developed at Fotomat (Japan)?

SUMMARY: When you're buying American, it's not just what you buy, it's where you buy it.

SHOP (cont.)

Gaston Jaunet (France)

Guy Laroche (France)

Honeybee (Germany)

Jaeger (UK)

Louis Feraud (France)

Louis Vuitton (France)

Miller's Outpost (Netherlands)

Revillon (France)

Saks Fifth Avenue (Bahrain)

Viyella (UK)

Wet Seal (Canada)

■ RETAIL STORES

Body Shop (UK)

Breuners (UK)

Color Tile (Bahrain)

Endicott Johnson (UK)

Fotomat (Japan)

Herman's Sporting Goods (UK)

Kay Jewelers (UK)

Pearle Vision Centers (UK)

Peoples Drug Store (Canada)

7-Eleven (Japan)

Universal Furniture (Hong Kong)

Vision Express (UK)

Watson's Personal Care Stores (Hong Kong)

■ SUPERMARKETS

A&P (Germany)

Bi-Lo (Netherlands)

Food Lion (Belgium)

Finast (Netherlands)

First National Supermarkets (Netherlands)

Giant Foods (Netherlands)

Liquor Barn (UK)

Park'n'Shop (Hong Kong)

Ralph's (Canada)

Shaws (UK)

Tops Markets (Netherlands)

Walbaums (Germany)

■ CLUBS/MAILING/ CATALOGS

BMG Music Service (Germany)

Columbia House Record & Tape (Japan)

Columbia TriStar Home Video (Japan)

Doubleday Book Club (Germany)

Spiegels Catalog (Germany)

■ AUCTION HOUSES

Christies (UK)

Sotheby's (UK)

■ HOUSEHOLD THINGS

Azko Salt (Netherlands)

Black Flag Roach Motel (UK)

Borateem (UK)

Brasso Metal Cleanser (UK)

Chore Boy (UK)

Cling Free Fabric Softener (Germany)

Cricket Neon Lighter (Switzerland)

Cutter Insect

Repellent (Germany)

Djeep Junior Lighter (France)

Drain Power (UK)

Durex Condom (UK)

Easy Off Oven Cleaner (UK)

Easy Wash (UK)

Evenflo Nipples (Venezuela)

Excita Condoms (UK)

Golden Fleece Scouring Pads (UK)

Gulf-Lite (UK)

Kiwi Shoe Polish (Australian)

Magic Mushroom (UK)

The Original Lime-A-Way (Germany)

Poulan Weed Eater (Sweden)

Ramses Condoms (UK)

Rug Fresh (UK)

Sani-Flush (UK)

Scripto Mighty Match (Japan)

Scrub Free (Germany)

S.O.S. (Germany)

Spray 'n Vac Rug Cleaners (UK)

Swish Toilet Bowl (UK)

20 Mule Team Borax (UK)

Wizard Air-Freshner (UK)

Wizard Charcoal Lighter (UK)

Yale Locks (UK)

SMELL
LIKE AN
AMERICAN

W hat does America smell like? Hamburgers sizzling on an open grill? A baseball stadium on opening day? Springtime in the Rocky Mountains? The New Jersey Turnpike?

If you chose "none of the above," you're right. The sad fact is that America no longer smells American at all.

Go to any big department store and follow your nose around the cosmetics section. Does it smell American to you? Check out the labels on those phallic perfume bottles. You'll see a lot names you can't pronounce. French names. Italian names. Dirty-sounding names.

What are Americans trying to cover up, you ask? Sweat and blood, that's what. The smells that made America great—a factory belching toxic fumes into the atmosphere, the pungent odor of armpits at work. The smell of industry. The smell of victory.

We used to be proud of that smell. Now every supermarket offers rows and rows of antiperspirants. What happened? It's simple: foreign companies convinced us that we smelled bad. Not surprisingly, they now dominate the $4.8 billion fragrance racket. Does anything smell Vichy to you?

SUMMARY: Each year consumers waste billions of dollars on fancy perfumes and colognes, only to wind up smelling un-American.

SMELL

L'Oreal (France)
Lou Lou
  (Switzerland)
Obsession
  (Netherlands/UK)
Opium (France)
Orlane (France)
Oscar de la Renta
  (France)
Paco Rabanne
  (Spain)
Paloma Picasso
  (Switzerland)
Pamerco
  (Switzerland)
Pierre Cardan
Polo (Switzerland)
Prince Matchabelli
  (Netherlands/UK)
Quintessence
  (Germany)
Ralph Lauren Safari
  (Switzerland)
Scherrer
  (Netherlands/UK)
Shalimar (France)
Shiseido (Japan)
Tigress
  (Netherlands/UK)
Tresor (Switzerland)
Verve
  (Netherlands/UK)
Vuarnet (France)
White Diamonds
  (Netherlands/UK)
White Shoulders
  (Netherlands/UK)

SHOP (cont.)

■ LAUNDRY AND
  DISHWASHING
  PRODUCTS
All Detergent
  (Netherlands/UK)
Calgon (Germany)
Electrasol
  (Germany)
Final Touch Fabric
  Softener
  (Netherlands/UK)
Jet Dry (Germany)
Rinso
  (Netherlands/UK)
Sunlight Soap
  (Netherlands/UK)
Surf
  (Netherlands/UK)
Snuggle
  (Netherlands/UK)
S.O.S. (Germany)
Sunlight
  (Netherlands/UK)
Wisk
  (Netherlands/UK)
Woolite (UK)
■ TOILETRIES
Adidas After Shave
  (Germany)
Aqua Velva After
  Shave (UK)
Bic Shavers (France)
Binaca Breath
  Spray (UK)
Calgon Bubble Bath
  (Germany)
Ciba Vision
  (Switzerland)
Clubman After
  Shave (UK)
Cutex Nail Polish
  (Netherlands/UK)
Dry Anti-Persperant
  (UK)
Faberge's Power
  Stick
  (Netherlands/UK)

Groom & Clean (UK)
Lady Powerstick
  (Netherlands/UK)
Lectric Shave (UK)
Magic Shaving
  Powder (UK)
Massengill Douche
  (UK)
Mentholatum
  Ointment (Japan)
Mr. Bubble (UK)
Oleg Cassini
  Manicure (UK)
Q-Tips
  (Netherlands/UK)
Sea & Ski Suntan
  Lotion
  (Netherlands/UK)
Shine On
  (Netherlands/UK)
Vaseline
  (Netherlands/UK)
Wilkinson Blades
  (Switzerland)
William's Mug
  Shaving Soap
  (UK)

48

PLAY
AMERICAN
SPORTS

Baseball, football, and basketball were America's gift to the world. And what have we gotten in return? A bunch of foreign-born players named Vlad and Manute.

Don't get us wrong—we have no objection to athletes coming here to make a buck, but it's a bad sign when they play our sports better than we do. For example, approximately 75 players in Major League baseball come from the Dominican Republic. That's nearly three players per team from one tiny Caribbean island.

Why are we being slam-dunked by the competition? Some say it's our lack of team spirit. They say Americans are too preoccupied with "sports" like windsurfing, sky diving, and bungee jumping to win one for the Gipper.

Ironically, the popularity of individual sports such as tennis and golf—both imported from the UK—comes at a time when American team sports are gaining acceptance throughout the world. So, it's not surprising that foreign investors, like their fellow athletes, sense a money-making opportunity in American sports.

Foreign ownership of American sports franchises is more than a political hot potato—it's a reality. Already, minor league baseball franchises such as the Birmingham Barons and the Salinas Spurs are being supported by foreign money.

SPORTS

■ SPORTING
   EQUIPMENT

Abu Garcia Fishing
   Gear (Sweden)

Bear Archery (UK)

Ben Hogan Golf
   (Japan)

Bridgestone
   Bicycles (Japan)

Connelly Skis
   (Germany)

Cycles Peugeot
   (France)

D & D Golf Balls
   (Finland)

Derby Bicycles
   (Luxembourg)

Dot Golf Balls
   (Venezuela)

Dunlop Tennis and
   Golf (UK)

Fuji Bicycles (Japan)

Gitane Bicycles
   (France)

Head Skis (Japan)

Jet Ski (Japan)

MacGregor (Finland)

Mizuno (Japan)

Prince Tennis (Italy)

ProStaff Golf
   (Finland)

Raleigh Bicycles
   (Luxembourg)

Rossignol Skis
   (France)

Skis Dynastar
   (France)

Spalding
   (Venezuela)

Tommy Armour Golf
   (UK)

Top-Flite Golf
   (Venezuela)

Universal Gym
   Equipment (UK)

49

SPORTS (cont.)

Valley Pool Tables (UK)

Wilson (Finland)

Yamaha (Japan)

■ ATHLETIC SHOES

Adidas (Germany)

Asics (Japan)

Etonic (Sweden)

Lotto (Italy)

Puma (Germany)

Tretorn (Sweden)

■ SPORTSWEAR

Bally of Switzerland (Switzerland)

Duofold (UK)

Eddie Bauer (Germany)

Head (Hong Kong)

North Face (Hong Kong)

Sierra Designs (Hong Kong)

Taylor Made (France)

And if we're not careful, our "national pastime" could soon be striking out for greener pastures.

SUMMARY: Americans now face stiff competition in their own sports. The solution? Smells like team spirit.

SPORTING GOODS

#1	Mizuno (Japan)
#2	Wilson (Finland)
#3	Titleist (USA)
#4	Spalding (Venezuela)
#5	Champion (USA)

Source: *Adweek's Marketing Week,* Superbrands, 1991

DUBIOUS ORIGINS: THE AMERICA'S CUP

The cup in the America's Cup is not made in America at all. Originally, the trophy was known in England as the Hundred-Guinea Cup. In 1851, the schooner *America* (which was later used in the Civil War by the Confederate Army) won the trophy for the New York Yacht Club. Afterwards, the competition was renamed the America's Cup and is now considered international yachting's top prize. Until recently, in fact, only Americans had won the America's Cup; however, in 1983, an Australian team became the first non-US crew to win the trophy. Incidentally, one hundred guineas, based on today's currency rates, is worth about $150.00.

PLAY
WITH
AMERICAN TOYS

Toys used to be simple and innocent. Little red wagons, Hula Hoops, and a sled named Rosebud were all we needed. Then train sets gave way to Matchbox cars (made in Hong Kong) and Lincoln Logs were replaced with Legos (made in Denmark).

Foreign influence spread so gradually in the toy industry that no one really noticed its extent until doctors began seeing kids with an entirely new injury: Nintendo Wrist. Like little lab rats on cocaine, our kids were playing these games until their paws were about ready to drop off.

Now, sociologists and teachers are worried about Nintendo Brain. They wonder what effect these games are having on our children's minds. Are we raising a generation of vidiots? We know the next generation won't lack airplane pilots, but will you want to trust your life to someone who's more familiar with Mario Brothers than the Wright Brothers?

More technologically advanced kids are beginning to speak a strange new language filled with references to Virtual Reality and Cyberspace. What does it all mean? No one knows. Except you get the sneaky feeling it's not a good sign for our literacy rate.

SUMMARY: Almost all of the video games mesmerizing our children in the $12 billion toy industry are made abroad. Drop the joystick and buy American toys.

TAKE
AN AMERICAN
VACATION

Americans spend $48.4 billion a year to travel outside this great land of ours. Fortunately for us, foreigners spend $59 billion a year to come here, creating a $10.6 billion surplus. In fact, tourism is now our largest industry.

This situation may not last much longer, however. Both the Europeans and Japanese have their own versions of our number-one tourist attraction, Disneyworld. And the Japanese are now talking about building something called a Presleyland in Tokyo to honor *our* King of Rock'n'Roll. As if visiting Graceland wasn't good enough!

If European and Japanese vacationers can have an American experience without actually coming here, then it's high time we did the same, don't you think? Forget Epcot Center—this summer, visit Euro-USA. Spend your dollars at home. Rent a canoe in Venice, Florida. Order some pasta in Rome, New York. Have a croissant in Paris, Texas (if you can find one).

Looking for a Middle Eastern adventure in the Midwest? Why not visit Cairo, Nebraska? Perhaps, you would prefer a religious experience? Make a pilgrimage to Mecca, California or Bethlehem, Pennsylvania.

Other travel options? Climb a wall in China, Maine; take a hike in Everest, Kansas and have some bubbly in Champaign, Illinois. If you get desperate, you could even sell your blue jeans in Moscow, Tennessee. Just stay in the USA. If you don't, you might as well go to Hell, Norway.

VACATION IN GUAM

If you've already been to Hawaii, Puerto Rico, and the US Virgin Islands and you're looking for another US territory to vacation in, look no further. Go to Guam.

Revel in the many attractions of this tiny West Pacific tropical paradise. Begin your day by rising out of bed to sing the national anthem, "Stand Ye Guamians." Don't worry—there's plenty more to do. Spend the morning sipping a piña colada while you drink in all 212 square miles of beautiful Guamian scenery.

Marvel at the fact that there are 12,000 snakes per square mile in Guam. Get out a calculator and figure out that there are 2,543,999 more snakes than you.

In recent years, Guam has become an extremely popular destination for Japanese tourists trying to avoid the crowds in Hawaii. In fact, 84 percent of all tourists in Guam are Japanese. That's okay—it still helps to offset our trade imbalance.

You'll be pleased to find that despite the little problem of taxation without representation, Guamians remain extremely patriotic. When the Phillipines didn't want our naval base, Guam welcomed us with open arms.

Next stop: the Bikini Islands.

SUMMARY: Why be treated like dirt in some far-off country when you can experience foreign travel in the USA? Fly to Mars (Pennsylvania). You won't even have to exchange your money.

VACATION (cont.)

Pebble Beach Golf Course (Japan)

Radio City Music Hall (Japan)

Rockefeller Center (Japan)

Snoeshow Ski Resort (Japan)

Steamboat Springs Ski Resort (Japan)

Stratton Mountain Ski Resort (Japan)

TropWorld Casino (Hong Kong)

Universal Studios Hollywood (Japan)

Universal Studios Florida (Japan)

■ RACETRACKS

Meadows, Pittsburgh, PA (UK)

Ladbroke, Detroit, MI (UK)

Golden Gate Fields, San Francisco (UK)

DRINK AMERICAN WATER

WATER

■ BOTTLED WATER

Arrowhead
(Switzerland)

Bandoit (France)

Belmont Springs
(Japan)

Calistoga (France)

Clearly Canadian
(Canada)

Evian (France)

Great Bear
(Switzerland)

Hinckley & Schmitt
(France)

Oasis (France)

Naya (Canada)

North Country
(Canada)

Poland Springs
(Switzerland)

Perrier (Switzerland)

Saint-Jean (France)

Saratoga Springs
(France)

Vittel (Switzerland)

Volvic (France)

Zephyr Hill Water
(France)

If water truly is "the most familiar and abundant liquid on earth," as the Columbia Encyclopedia claims it is, then why do Americans spend $2.65 billion a year to buy it? Water is not exactly hard to find. In fact, it covers 70 percent of the Earth's surface.

And, yet, for some unexplained reason, a few French companies have managed to monopolize the American bottled water market. Since water is our most precious bodily fluid—making up 80 percent of a person's muscle tissue and 92 percent of blood plasma—perhaps we should begin to question what we're pouring down our collective throats.

The French, after all, will ingest just about anything. These are the people who believe that eating *foie gras* (diseased goose livers) can reduce the risk of heart disease, and that *cervelles au beurre noir* (calf's brain in brown butter sauce) is a delicacy. We won't even mention Jerry Lewis.

Recently, a high-profile French-owned water company had to recall bottles contaminated with benzene, a poisonous liquid that causes cancer in lab animals. (At least, they're not just picking on us—Japan suspended imports of French mushrooms suspected of having radiation contamination from Chernobyl.)

SUMMARY: Health-conscious Americans are drinking more bottled water than ever. Ironically, they are trusting the French to supply it.

WE'RE
NOT ALONE

In a global economy, loyalty for the sake of patriotism is often an exercise in frustration. As a consequence of mergers and acquisitions, ownership keeps changing while brand names remain the same.

If you think consumers in the USA have suffered a disproportionate share of slings and arrows in this regard, consider the chagrin to our neighbors to the north who must live with the fact that both Canada Dry and Canadian Club are owned by corporations based in the United Kingdom.

The British are hardly immune. When Princess Diana traded in her British-made Jaguar for a German Mercedes-Benz, a royal fuss was made in England's tabloid press. But they weren't exactly laughing over in Germany since Bayer aspirin, a local invention, lost its patent in the USA (it is now sold by an American-based company that uses its name).

Next door in France, Perrier, the world-famous mineral water company and source of much Gallic pride, was recently sold to Swiss-based Nestlés. One gets the feeling, the citizens of Switzerland probably do not feel neutral, however, about Swiss Miss hot chocolate. You guessed it—it's made in America.

SUMMARY: We're all in this together, whether we like it or not.

FEATURES

THE CANADIAN
CONSPIRACY

What do you mean, *what* Canadian conspiracy? How else does a country with a population one-tenth of ours manage to control so many of our vital economic and cultural institutions?

Did you know, for example, that the largest foreign investor in the US, Joseph E. Seagram & Sons, was begun by a Canadian bootlegger who smuggled whiskey over the border during Prohibition? Does it surprise you that real estate developers Olympia & York, based in Canada, are the biggest landlords in Manhattan?

Did you realize that one in ten domestic "American" cars is actually made in Canada? That 750,000 US citizens are employed by Canada-based companies? Is it merely a coincidence that the anthem of a popular Canadian rock band was "Takin' Care of Business?"

Did you know that Canadians are responsible for Harlequin Romance novels and much of our airplane food (Sky Chefs)? And exactly *how* did Canada come to own half of Niagara Falls anyway?

Do you believe—as some do—that the big debate on Capitol Hill over jobs moving to Mexico is just a red herring, to throw us off the Canadian trail and prevent a wave of Canada-bashing? Do they realize that it isn't working? Have you heard the one about the three Canadian deer hunters?

SUMMARY: Do you believe a red flannel menace is rising to the north? Aren't you concerned that you can't pick them out in a crowd?

THE MEDIA
CONSPIRACY

Inquiring minds want to know: Is there a media conspiracy? Who really controls what we read, see, and hear? Do you believe that outside influences could penetrate the powerful corridors of television networks?

Did you know that media baron Rupert Murdoch—whose Australia-based News Corporation owns both the Fox TV network and *TV Guide*—has changed his citizenship from Australian to American in order to meet FCC standards for television station ownership?

How about the fact that UK-based Reed Publishing owns both *Broadcasting* magazine and *Publishers Weekly*? Is it just a coincidence that influential periodicals like the *Financial Times* and *The Economist* are also published in England?

Was the late English mogul Robert Maxwell, who rescued the *New York Daily News,* really good 'til the last drop?

Is it significant that more than 100 of America's daily newspapers are owned by Thomson Corporation, a huge media conglomerate headquartered in Canada, which also publishes the bible of military information, *Jane's Defence Weekly*?

And what about the *New York Times*? Can they really print the "paper of record" on the paper of Canada?

Have you heard about Toshiba buying 12.5 percent ownership in Time Warner Entertainment? Is it true that producers at Japanese-owned Universal Studios changed the script for Tom Selleck's movie *Mr. Baseball* to make it appear more pro-Japanese?

SUMMARY: Is it possible that Big Brother has already come to a theater near you?

MEDIA (cont.)

WNYW NY (Australia)

WTTG Washington DC (Australia)

■ NEWSPAPERS

Boston Herald (Australia)

San Antonio Express News (Australia)

Financial Times (UK)

Daily Variety (UK)

■ MAGAZINES

American Baby (UK)

American Banker (Canada)

Audio (France)

TV Guide (Australia)

Beauty (France)

Boating (France)

Broadcasting (UK)

Car and Driver (France)

Cycle World (France)

Design News (UK)

Digital Review (UK)

Economist (UK)

Elle (France)

First for Women (Germany)

Flying (France)

Frequent Flyer Magazine (UK)

Home (France)

Interior Design (UK)

Jane's Defence Weekly

Jenny Craig's Your Body, Your Health (France)

Major League Baseball Official Preview (France)

Mirabella (Australia)

Modern Bride (UK)

Parents (Germany)

Popular Photography (France)

Power & Motoryacht (UK)

Publisher's Weekly (UK)

Restaurants and Institutions (UK)

Road and Track (France)

Sail (UK)

Scientific American (Germany)

Showboats International (France)

Stereo Review (France)

Travel Weekly (UK)

TV Guide (Australia)

Woman's Day (France)

Woman's World (Germany)

Variety (UK)

Woman's World (Germany)

THE BUY
AMERICA
HALL OF SHAME

T he Buy America Hall of Shame showcases those individuals and corporations who have knowingly violated the good will of citizens and supporters of the "Buy America" crusade for the benefit of their bank balance or cheap publicity. A top ten list of offenders follows, and each inductee is dishonored with a personalized Hall of Shame prize.

HALL OF SHAME TOP TEN

#1	The Ming Teh Flag Company
#2	Wal-Mart
#3	US Department of Agriculture
#4	Ronald Reagan
#5	Honda
#6	The Tan Family
#7	Beth Ann Herman/Maserati
#8	Georgette Mosbacher
#9	US Postal Service
#10	Lee Greenwood

INDUCTEE: The Ming Teh Flag Company

An advertisement mailed to US flagmakers in 1987 by the Ming Teh Flag Company of Taipei, Taiwan, suggested that potential buyers of their imported American flags should replace the tag "Made in Taiwan" with a phony "Made in the USA" label.

After acknowledging the reason for removing the label—to prevent the resistance in U.S. to import flags—the ad goes on to instruct companies on how to achieve this effect: "We suggest you cut off this label after you receive the goods and spend very little cost to mark on the flags your own brand name and Made in the U.S.A. signs."

The resulting flap led Congressman Harley O. Staggers, Jr. (D-WV) to introduce the American Flag Fidelity Act—banning the importation of US flags—in 1991.

HALL OF SHAME PRIZE: A Taiwanese flag made in America.

INDUCTEE: Wal-Mart

When the late Sam Walton launched Wal-Mart's "Buy America" campaign in 1985 he announced the company was "firmly committed to the philosophy of buying everything possible from suppliers who manufacture their products in the United States." By 1992, Wal-Mart was taking credit for saving 60,347 American jobs.

A closer look at the country's largest retailer, however, reveals glaring exceptions to their committment. Some industry analysts have estimated that 25-30% of Wal-Mart's goods are imported. Examples: fourteen styles of Wal-Mart's private-label, trademarked boots and shoes were produced in China, the company operates buying offices in both Taiwan and Hong Kong, and 72.1% of their photo processing car fleet is Mazdas.

Apparently, the company's new president, Rob Walton is less committed to "Buy American" than his dad: he already owns nine foreign-made cars.

HALL OF SHAME PRIZE: An American flag supplied by the Ming Teh Flag Company of Taiwan.

INDUCTEE: The US Department of Agriculture

As part its $200-million-a-year Market Promotion Program, the US Department of Agriculture supplies grants to help farmers promote their products for export. In 1991, the Associated Press reported that several million of these dollars had been earmarked for major food corporations such as McDonalds, Campbell's, and Hershey that already have substantial advertising budgets.

At least two beneficiaries of this program were foreign-owned corporations: Burger King (owned by UK-based Grand Metropolitan) and Canadian-based Joseph E. Seagram & Sons, which received $146,000 to promote Four Roses whiskey.

HALL OF SHAME PRIZE: A rotten tomato.

INDUCTEE: Ronald Reagan

In 1989, ex-President Ronald Reagan was paid $2,000,000 (or $50,000 a minute) for two twenty-minute speeches he delivered to the Fujisankei Communications Group in Japan. His total earnings from the two speeches was $400,000 more than he earned in eight years as President.

During his trip to Japan, Reagan was asked his opinion on Sony Corporation's then-recent purchase of Columbia Pictures. His response: "Maybe Hollywood needs some outsiders to bring back decency and good taste to some of the pictures being made."

Coincidentally, representatives of Reagan's presidential library had been negotiating with Sony for a contribution of electronic or video equipment to the library.

The *New York Times* later reported that, while in Japan, Reagan participated in several fund-raising efforts for the library including a "friendship concert" in Yokohama featuring Perry Como and

Placido Domingo attended by 17,000 Japanese citizens.

HALL OF SHAME PRIZE: A collection of Kitty Kelly books for the Reagan Library.

INDUCTEE: Honda

Not content to have the bestselling car (the Honda Accord) in the USA for three years running, Honda company executives decided to test their luck in early 1992 with an advertising campaign featuring the slogan, "Who says 'Made in the U.S.A.' doesn't cut it anymore?"

The ad, which appeared in newspapers such as the *Washington Post,* stressed pride in the "skilled...associates" who "carefully" assemble lawn mowers at Honda's Swepsonville, North Carolina plant. Later, the ad emphasizes that many of these lawn mowers are "being exported to destinations as distant as France and Japan."

The logic? We, as Americans, are supposed to feel pride that Americans working for Japanese companies are outperforming Americans working for American companies.

HALL OF SHAME PRIZE: A giant lawn job for the company with "the car that sells itself."

INDUCTEE: The Tan Family

In early 1992, the US Department of Labor filed suit against Tan Enterprises for alleged labor violations—including unpaid wages and sweatshop-like working conditions—in their clothing manufacturing plant, the American International Knitter Corporation, located in Saipan, a US possession in the western Pacific.

Due to its location, the Tans—and the companies that used their services—were legally permitted to stitch "Made in the USA" on the labels of their products. Companies working with Tan prior to the allegations included Perry Ellis, LaMonde, Eddie Bauer, Chaps Sportswear, Christian Dior, Levi Strauss, and Van Heusen.

HALL OF SHAME PRIZE: Five to ten years of hard labor in Club Fed.

INDUCTEE: Beth Ann Herman/Maserati

In 1989, the *New York Times* reported that writer Beth Ann Herman had received compensation for mentioning Maserati in her book *Power City*—the first documented case of a product placement in a novel.

In exchange for her Maserati advertisement ("The V-6 engine has two turbochargers, 185 horsepower, and got up to 60 in under seven seconds"), Herman received a $15,000 party thrown at a Maserati dealership in Beverly Hills which drew press coverage from CNN and *Entertainment Tonight*.

HALL OF SHAME PRIZE: A book featuring a passage about a writer named Beth Ann Herman taking out a loan to pay for her Maserati's transmission troubles.

INDUCTEE: Georgette Mosbacher

Georgette Mosbacher should know about inside the Beltway diplomacy—after all, her husband, Robert Mosbacher (described as "a caricature of the fatuous and overstuffed plutocrat" by *Harpers* magazine) was George Bush's Secretary of Commerce and later the chairman of his 1992 reelection campaign.

Nevertheless, Ms. Mosbacher was overheard by *Newsweek* magazine in late 1991 making the following indiscreet comment after her husband took the latter job: "I just can't wait till this campaign is over so I can say, 'Bob, open the garage door and get out the Maserati! Open up the safe and get out the jewels.' "

Adding irony to injury: Ms. Mosbacher and a group of investors had just netted a cool $10 million by selling off their cosmetics company, La Prairie, to a German-owned firm. Now you know why they call it the Commerce Department.

HALL OF SHAME PRIZE: The same Maserati troubles as Beth Ann Herman.

INDUCTEE: The US Postal Service

In March, 1991, the *Washington Post* reported that a stamp honoring the late Senator Dennis Chavez— the first American-born Hispanic in the Senate— had been printed in Canada. The reason given by Postal Service officials for exporting the job was the lack of a particular kind of printing press in the United States. Ironically, the 35-cent stamp was part of the "Great Americans" series.

HALL OF SHAME PRIZE: A sackful of protest letters sent postage due from stamp collectors.

INDUCTEE: Lee Greenwood

Who can forget country singer Lee Greenwood's stirring rendition of his patriotic anthem "God Bless The USA" performed at football halftime shows during the Gulf War?

Certainly, not the CEOs of MCA and Polygram. The reason? The recording of "God Bless The USA" is released by Japanese-owned MCA Records. The publishing rights are controlled by Dutch-owned Polygram. Both companies were, no doubt, overjoyed to have all the free publicity.

Greenwood recently switched labels from MCA to Liberty Records, which sounds like a patriotic move, until you realize that the label is owned by Capitol Records, which is based in England. Nice try, Lee.

HALL OF SHAME PRIZE: A bilingual version of "God Bless Lee Greenwood" sung in Japanese.

LENNY BRUCE'S
PATRIOTIC
TEST

Where do you draw the line as a patriotic consumer? Every person has their threshold—some have a weakness for fancy foreign chocolates, others for luxury sedans.

There are countless pitfalls and temptations. Is it really un-American to vacation abroad, play video games, or enjoy a good French wine? You must be the judge of your own behavior. Each time you go shopping, you are testing your limits.

With that in mind, we leave the last word to Lenny Bruce, who addressed this complicated issue in his classic autobiography, *How to Talk Dirty and Influence People.*

I love my country, I would give allegiance to no other nation, nor would I choose any other for my home, and yet if I followed a U.S. serviceman and saw the enemy bind him, nude, face down, and then pour white-hot lead into a funnel that was inserted in his keister, they wouldn't even have to heat another pot for me. I would give them every top secret, I would make shoeshine rags out of the American flag, I would denounce the Constitution, I would give them the right to kill every person that was kind and dear to me. Just don't give me that hot-lead enema.

QUICK REFERENCE
GUIDE TO FOREIGN-OWNED BRANDS

A

A.B. Dick Office Equipment (UK)

A&M Records (Netherlands)

A&P Supermarkets (Germany)

AEG Olympia Photography (Germany)

Abbots Old Philadelphia Ice Cream (Canada)

Abraham & Strauss (Canada)

Absolut Vodka (Sweden)

Abu Garcia Fishing Gear (Sweden)

Actifed Antihistamine (UK)

Acutrim Appetite Suppressant (Switzerland)

Acura Integra Automobile (Japan)

Adidas Aftershave (Germany)

Adidas Athletic Shoes (Germany)

Adolph's Meat Tenderizer (Netherlands/UK)

Advantage Hair Coloring (Switzerland)

After Eight (Switzerland)

Agfa Photography (Germany)

Aim Toothpaste (Netherlands/UK)

Aiwa Electronics (Japan)

Akai Electronics (Japan)

Alert Antiperspirant (Netherlands/UK

Alexandra De Markoff Cosmetics (France)

Alfa Romeo Automobiles (Italy)

Alfred Dunhill of London (UK)

Alka-Seltzer Antacid (Germany)

All Detergent (Netherlands/UK)

All In One Shampoo (Netherlands/UK)

Alladin Hotel and Casino (Japan)

Allied Vans (UK)

All Ready Pie Crusts (UK)

Almond Chocolate (Japan)

Alpine White (Switzerland)

Alpo Pet Foods (UK)

Altoids Candy (UK)

Amaretto di Saronno (Italy)

Ambassador Scotch (UK)

Ambre Beige Nail Polish (Switzerland)

Amstel Beer (Netherlands)

Amiga Personal Computer (Japan)

Anais Anais (Switzerland)

Anchor Brush (Netherlands)

Andover Cigarettes (UK)

Appleton Rums (UK)

Aqua-Fresh Toothpaste (UK)

Aqua Net Hairspray (Netherlands/UK)

Aqua Velva Aftershave (UK)

Aramis Cologne (France)

Arista Records (Germany)

Armitron Watches (Japan)

Arrowhead Bottled Water (Switzerland)

Arrow Shirts (France)

Asahi Beer (Japan)

Asics Footwear (Japan)

Aston Martin Automobile (UK)

Atari Lynx Video System (Japan)

Audi Automobile (Germany)

Aunt Nellie's Farm Kitchens(UK)

Aziza Cosmetics
(Netherlands/UK)

Azko Salt (Netherlands)

B

BASF Tape (Germany)

BMG Music Service (Germany)

BMW Automobile (Germany)

Baby Ruth Candy Bar
(Switzerland)

Baci Chocolates (Switzerland)

Bactine Antiseptic (Germany)

Baileys Original Irish Cream
(Ireland)

Ballantine's Scotch (UK)

Bally of Switzerland
(Switzerland)

Bang and Olufsen Stereo
Equipment (Denmark)

Bantam Books (Germany)

Baskin-Robbins (UK)

Bear Archery (UK)

Becks Beer (Germany)

Beefeater Gin (England)

Belair Cigarettes (UK)

Bell's Scotch (Scotland)

Belmont Springs Water (Japan)

Benedictine Liqueur (UK)

Ben Hogan Golf (Japan)

Benihana Restuarant (Japan)

Benetton Apparel (Italy)

Bentley Automobile (UK)

Beretta Guns (Italy)

Bergin Line (Norway)

Bernardi Italian Foods (UK)

Bertolli Olive Oil (Italy)

Best Friend Pet Food (Australia)

Bic Shavers/Lighters/Pens
(France)

Big Balloon Bubble Gum (Japan)

Bigelow Tea (UK)

Binaca Breath Spray (UK)

Bit-O-Honey Candy (Switzerland)

Black Cat Cigarettes (UK)

Black Flag Roach Motel (UK)

Black Velvet Whiskey (UK)

Bloomingdale's Department
Store (Canada)

Blaupunkt Car Radios (Germany)

Blue Mountain Pet Food (UK)

Bohemia Beer (Mexico)

Bombay Gin (England)

Bon Bon Nuggets (Switzerland)

Boodles Gin (Canada)

Borateem Borax (UK)

Borkum Riff Tobacco (Sweden)

Boursin Cheese (France)

Brasso Metal Cleanser (UK)

Breckenridge Ski Resort (Japan)

Breitling Watches (Switzerland)

Bridgestone Tires (Japan)

Bright Eyes Pet Food (UK)

British Petroleum (UK)

Brooks Brothers Apparel (UK)

Brother Electronics (Japan)

Brylcreem Hairdressing
Products (UK)

Buffet Pet Food (Switzerland)

Bugler Tobacco (UK)

Bugs Bunny Vitamins (Germany)

Bulgari Jewelry (Italy)

Bumble Bee Tuna (Thailand)

Burberry Apparel (UK)

Burger King Fast-food
Restaurant (UK)

Bustelo Coffee (UK)

Butler Dental Floss (Japan)

Butterfinger Candy Bar
(Switzerland)

Butternut Candy Bar (Finland)

C

CBS Records (Japan)

Cain's Coffee (Switzerland)

Calgon Bubble Bath (Germany)

Calistoga Bottled Water (France)

Callard & Bowser English Toffee (UK)

Calvin Klein's Obsession (Netherlands/UK)

Calvert Extra Whiskey (Canada)

Campari Liqueur (Italy)

Canada Dry Soft Drink (UK)

Canadian Club Whiskey (Canada)

Canadian Hunter Whiskey (Canada)

Canon Electronics (Japan)

Capitol Records (UK)

Captain Morgan Rum (Canada)

Capri Cigarettes (UK)

Car and Driver Magazine (France)

Caress Soap (Netherlands/UK)

Carnation Hot Cocoa (Switzerland)

Carr's Table Water Crackers (UK)

Carvel Ice Cream (Bahrain)

Casio Electronics (Japan)

Castrol Oil (UK)

Cattleman's Bar-B-Q (UK)

Cellini Watches (Switzerland)

Chanel Perfume (French)

Chase and Sanborn Coffee (Switzerland)

Chef's Bland Pet Food (Switzerland)

Chivas Regal Scotch (UK)

Chloe Fragrance (Netherlands/UK)

Choc-O-Malt Ice Cream (Switzerland)

Chocks Vitamins (Germany)

Chore Boy Pot Cleaner (UK)

Chryalis Records (Japan)

Chuckles Candy (Finland)

Chunky Candy (Switzerland)

Ciba Vision Contact Lens Care (Switzerland)

Cinzano Vermouth (Italy)

Citgo Gasoline (Venezuela)

Citizen Watches (Japan)

Clamato Beverage (UK)

Clan MacGregor Scotch (Scotland)

Clarins Cosmetics (France)

Clarion Electronics (Japan)

Clean & Smooth Soap (Germany)

Clearly Canadian Bottled Water (Canada)

Cling Free Fabric Softener (Germany)

Close-Up Toothpaste (Netherlands/UK)

Club Cocktails (UK)

Club Crackers (UK)

Clubman After-shave (UK)

Club Med (France)

Coffee-Mate Non-dairy Creamer (Switzerland)

Collier's Encyclopedia (UK)

Colombo Frozen Yogurt (France)

Color Tile (Bahrain)

Columbia Pictures (Japan)

Columbia Records (Japan)

Columbia House Record & Tape (Japan)

Columbia TriStar Home Video (Japan)

Come 'N Get It Pet Food (Switzerland)

Connoisseur Tuna Fish (Canada)

Contac Cold Remedy (UK)

Contadina Pasta (Switzerland)

Continental Tires (Germany)

Corgi Model Cars (UK)

Corona Beer (Mexico)

Cote d'Or Chocolates (Spain)

Courvoisier Cognac (UK)

Crabtree and Evelyn (UK)

Creamsicle Ice Cream (Netherlands/UK)

Cricket Neon Lighter
(Switzerland)

Crosse & Blackwell Sauces
(Switzerland)

Crown Royal Whiskey (Canada)

Crystal Palace Vodka (UK)

Cunard Line (UK)

Cup-A-Soup (Netherlands/UK)

Cup O'Noodles (Japan)

Cutex Nail Polish
(Netherlands/UK)

Cutter Insect Repellent
(Germany)

Cutty Sark Scotch (Scotland)

Cycle World Magazine (France)

Cycles Peugeot Bicycles
(France)

D

DAK Ham (Denmark)

Dannon Yogurt (France)

D & D Golf Balls (Finland)

Decca Records (Netherlands)

Delicious Vinyl Records
(Netherlands)

Dell Books (Germany)

Del Monte Food Products (UK)

Denon Audio Equipment (Japan)

Derby Bicycles (Luxembourg)

Derma-Soft Creme (Switzerland)

Design Hair Care (Germany)

Deutsche Grammophon
Records (Netherlands)

De Ville Brandy (France)

Dewar's Scotch (UK)

Diahatsu Automobiles (Japan)

Dillard Department Stores
(Netherlands)

Djeep Lighters (France)

Doan's Analgesic (Switzerland)

Dolce and Gabbana Fashion
(Italy)

Domino Sugar (UK)

Dos Equis Beer (Mexico)

Dot Golf Balls (Venezuela)

Doubleday & Co. Books
(Germany)

Dove Soap (Netherlands/UK)

Drain Power Drain-clog Remover
(UK)

Drakkar Noir Cologne
(Switzerland)

Dr. Maartens Shoes (UK)

Dreyer's Grand Ice Cream
(Bahamas)

Drum Tobacco (Holland)

Drumstick Sundae Cone
(Switzerland)

Dry Antipersperant (UK)

Duggan's Dew Scotch
(Scotland)

Dunes Casino (Japan)

Dulcolax Laxative (Germany)

Dunkin' Donuts (UK)

Dunlop Tires (Japan)

Dunlop Tennis and Golf (UK)

Durango Boots (UK)

Durex Condoms (UK)

Durkee French Foods (Australia)

E

EMI Records (UK)

Easy Off Oven Cleaner (UK)

Easy-Wash Laundry Detergent
(UK)

Economist Magazine (UK)

Ecotrin Analgesic (UK)

Eddie Bauer Clothing (Germany)

Elizabeth Arden Cosmetics
(Netherlands/UK)

Elizabeth Taylor's Passion
(Netherlands/UK)

Elkes Biscuits Cookies (UK)

El Pico Coffee (UK)

Elle Magazine (France)

Endicott Johnson Footwear (UK)

Epic Records (Japan)

Epson Computers (Japan)

Erno Laszlo Skin-care Products
(Netherlands/UK)

Eternity Fragrance
(Netherlands/UK)
Etienne Aigner Shoes (France)
Etonic Shoes (Sweden)
Eureka Vacuum Cleaners
(Sweden)
Evenflo Nipples (Venezuela)
Eversoft Skin Moisturizer
(Japan)
Evian Mineral Water (France)
Excita Condoms (UK)
Ex-Lax Laxative (Switzerland)

F

Faberge Fragrences
(Netherlands/UK)
Factory Records (UK)
Falcon Men's Hairspray (UK)
Familia Cereal (Switzerland)
Fancy Feast Cat Food
(Switzerland)
Fanny Farmer Candy (France)
Farberware Cookware (UK)
Feline Pet Food (Switzerland)
Fendi Fragrance
(Netherlands/UK)
Ferrari Automobiles (Italy)
Ferrero Mon Cheri Candy (Italy)
Final Touch Fabric Softener
(Netherlands/UK)
Financial Times Newspaper (UK)
Finlandia Vodka (Finland)
Firestone Tires (Japan)
First for Women Magazine
(Germany)
First National Supermarkets
(Netherlands)
Fisherman's Friend Cough
Remedy (UK)
Fleischmann's Preferred
Whiskey (UK)
Fleischmann's Yeast (Australia)
Fletcher's Castoria Laxative
(Japan)
Flintstones Vitamins (Germany)

Flying Magazine (France)
Fontana Records (Netherlands)
Foster's Ale (Australia)
Fotomat Photofinishing Service
(Japan)
4th and Broadway Records
(Netherlands)
Free & Lovely Antidandruff
Foam (UK)
Frequent Flyer Magazine (UK)
Fresh Catch Cat Food
(Switzerland)
Fridgidaire Refrigerators
(Sweden)
Friskies Pet Food (Switzerland)
Frye Boots (UK)
Fuji Photographic Supplies
(Japan)
Fujica Electronics (Japan)
Fujitsu Car Stereos (Japan)

G

Gas-X Antacid (Switzerland)
Geffen Records (Japan)
General Tires (Germany)
Genie Garage-door Openers
(Netherlands)
Georgia Boots (UK)
Geritol Vitamin Supplement (UK)
CIGA Hotels (Italy)
Gianni Versace Tiles (France)
Giant Foods Supermarkets
(Netherlands)
Gibson Appliances (Sweden)
Gilbey's Gin (England)
Giorgio Armani Fragrance
(Switzerland)
Girbaud Apparel (France)
Gitane Cigarettes (France)
Glenlivet Scotch (Canada)
Glenmore Scotch (UK)
Gloria Vanderbilt Fragrance
(Switzerland)
Gold Blend Coffee (Switzerland)

Golden Fleece Scouring Pads (UK)

Goldstar Electronics (Korean)

Goobers Candy (Switzerland)

Good Humor Ice Cream (UK)

Good 'n Fruity Candy (Finland)

Good & Plenty Candy (Finland)

Gordon's Gin (England)

Gordon's Vodka (UK)

Grand Gourmet Dog Food (Switzerland)

Grand Marnier Liqueur (France)

Grandma's Molasses (UK)

Great Bear Water (Switzerland)

Green Giant Vegetables (UK)

Grolsch Beer (Netherlands)

Gucci Luggage (Italy)

Guinness Stout (Ireland)

Guiness Museum of World Records (UK)

Gulf-Lite Charcoal Starter (UK)

G-U-M Toothbrush (Japan)

Guy Laroche Fragrance (France)

H

Häagen-Dazs Ice Cream (UK)

Haller Clock (Germany)

Halsey Taylor Drinking Foundtains (UK)

Hamilton Watches (Switzerland)

Hard Rock Cafe (UK)

Hardees Restaurant Franchise (Canada)

Harlequin Romance Novels (Canada)

Harp Lager Beer (Ireland)

HarperCollins Books (Australia)

Harvey's Bristol Cream Sherry (England)

Hasselblad Photographic Equipment (Germany)

Head Sportswear (Hong Kong)

Heath Bars Candy (Finland)

Heineken Beer (Netherlands)

Helene Curtis Cosmetics (France)

Hennessy Cognac (UK)

Herb Ox Boullion Cubes (Australia)

Henry Holt Books (Germany)

Herman's Sporting Goods (UK)

Heublein Alcoholic Beverages (UK)

Heuer Stopwatches (Switzerland)

Highland Piper Scotch (Scotland)

Hills Brothers Coffee (Switzerland)

Hilton International Hotels (UK)

Hinckley & Schmitt Water (France)

Hires Root Beer (UK)

Hitachi Electronics (Japan)

Hoegh Lines (Norway)

Hohner Harmonicas (Germany)

Holiday Inn Hotels (UK)

Holland House Cooking Wine (UK)

Holsten Beer (Germany)

Honda Automobiles (Japan)

HOME Magazine (France)

Honeywell/Bull Computers (France)

Horlick's Malted Milk (UK)

Howard Johnson's Food Products (UK)

Hungry Jack Rolls (UK)

Hyundai Automobiles (Korea)

I

IKEA Home Furnishings (Sweden)

IRS Records (Netherlands)

I Can't Believe It's Not Butter Margarine (UK)

Imperial Margarine (Netherlands/UK)

Imperial Tobacco (Canada)

Impulse Body Spray (Netherlands/UK)

Infiniti Automobiles (Japan)

Inter-continental Hotels (Japan)

Interior Design Magazine (UK)

Inver House Scotch (UK)

Island Records (Netherlands)

Isuzu Automobiles (Japan)

J

J&B Scotch (Scotland)

Jacuzzi (UK)

Jaeger Apparel (UK)

Jameson Whiskey (Ireland)

Jane's Defence Weekly Magazine (Canada)

Jenny Craig's Your Body, Your Health Magazine (France)

Jeno's Pizza (UK)

Jergens Soap (Japan)

Jet Dry Rinse Additive (German)

Jet Ski Marine Vehicle (Japan)

JetVac Vacuum Cleaners (Netherlands)

Job Bleu Cigarettes (France)

John Courage Beer (England)

John Henry Chewing Tobacco (UK)

John Player Scotch (UK)

Johnnie Walker Scotch (Scotland)

Jolly Rancher Candy (Finland)

Jordan Marsh (Canada)

Jose Cuervo Tequila (Mexico)

Jovan Musk Perfume (Germany)

Just Wonderful Hair-care Products (Netherlands/UK)

JVC Electronics (Japan)

K

Kahlua Liqeur (UK)

Kawai Musical Instruments (Japan)

Kawasaki Motorcylces (Japan)

Kay Jewelers (UK)

Keebler Crackers and Cookies (UK)

Kellogg's Castor Oil (UK)

Kelvinator Appliances (Sweden)

Kenwood Electronics (Japan)

Kern's Fruit Juices (Switzerland)

Kessler Whiskey (Canada)

Kikkoman Sauces (Japan)

Kingfisher Beer (India)

Kirin Beer (Japan)

Kite Tobacco (UK)

Kiwi Shoe-care Products (Australian)

Knox Gelatine (Netherlands/UK)

Konica Cameras (Japan)

Kool Cigarettes (UK)

Kronenbourg Beer (France)

Krups Appliances (Germany)

L

Labatt's Beer (Canada)

Lady Powerstick (Netherlands/UK)

Lagerfeld Hair-care Products (Netherlands/UK)

Lancome Cosmetics (Switzerland)

La Prairie Skin-care Products (Germany)

Laura Ashley Apparel (UK)

Lauren Fragrance (Switzerland)

Lawry's Seasoned Salt (Netherlands/UK)

La Yogurt (Canada)

Lazarus Department Sore (Canada)

Lea & Perrins Worchester Sauce (France)

Leading Edge Computers (Japan)

Lean Cuisine Frozen Entrees (Switzerland)

Lectric Shave Shaving Products (UK)

Lego System (Denmark)

Leica Cameras (Switzerland)

Leroux Liqueur (Canada)

Lesueur Peas (UK)

Letraset Graphic Arts Materials (Sweden)

Lever 2000 Soap (Netherlands/UK)

Lexus Automobile (Japan)

Libby's Fruit Juices (Switzerland)

Liberty Records (UK)

Lifebuoy Soap (Netherlands/UK)

Lindt Chocolate (Switzerland)

Lipton Tea/Soup (Netherlands/UK)

Liquor Barn (UK)

Liv-A-Snaps Pet Food (UK)

London Records (Netherlands)

Lord Calvert Whiskey (Canada)

L'Oreal Hair (France)

Lotte Chewing Gum (Japan)

Lotto Footwear (Italy)

Lotus Automobiles (UK)

Louis Feraud Fragrance (France)

Louis Sherry Ice Cream (Canada)

LouLou Fragrance (Switzerland)

Lucky Eggs Candy (Italy)

Lux Soap (Netherlands/UK)

M

MCA Records (Japan)

MGM-Pathe Films (France)

MJB Coffee (Switzerland)

Maalox Antacid (France)

Mac Baren Pipe Tobacco (Denmark)

MacGregor Sporting Goods (Finland)

Mack Trucks (France)

Maclean Toothpaste (UK)

Macmillan Books (UK)

Magic Mushroom Air Freshener (UK)

Magic Shaving Powder (UK)

Magnavox Electronics (Netherlands)

Malibu Musk Fragrance (France)

Malted Milk Eggs Candy (Finland)

Mango Records (Netherlands)

Manhattan Records (UK)

Marshall Fields (UK)

Martell Cognac (Canada)

Maserati Automobiles (Italy)

Massengill Douche (UK)

MasterCare Auto Service Centers (Japan)

Maxell Tape (Japan)

Mazda Automobiles (Japan)

McEwan's Ale (England)

Medaglia d'Or Coffee (UK)

Medi-Quick First-aid Ointment (Japan)

Meineke Discount Muffler Shop (UK)

Memorex Tape (Netherlands)

Mentholatum Ointment (Japan)

Mentos Candy (Netherlands)

Mercedes-Benz Automobiles (Germany)

Mercury Records (Netherlands)

Meridien Hotels (France)

Mermaid Table Salt (UK)

Metaprel Asthma Treatment (Switzerland)

Metaxa Liqueur (Greece)

Michelin Tires (France)

Mighty Dog Pet Food (Switzerland)

Milk Duds Candy (Finland)

Milk Shake Candy (Finland)

Minolta Photographic Equipment (Japan)

Mirabella Magazine (Australia)

Mister Donut (UK)

Mister Softee (UK)

Mita Photocopiers (Japan)

Mitchell's Apple Sauce (UK)

Mitsubishi Automobiles (Japan)

Mizuno Sporting Goods (Japan)

Modern Bride Magazines (UK)
Modern Maid Four Mixes (UK)
Mohawk Tires (Japan)
Molson Ale (Canada)
Mom's Margarine
(Netherlands/UK)
Moët & Chandon Champagne
(France)
Monogram Hobby Kits (UK)
Mont Blanc Pens (Germany)
Montezuma Tequila (Mexico)
Moosehead Beer (Canada)
Morgan Creek Records
(Netherlands)
Motel 6 Motel Chain (France)
Mott's Apple Sauce (UK)
Mr. Bubble Bathing Soap (UK)
Mrs. Butterworth Maple Syrup
(Netherlands/UK)
Mrs. Filbert's Margarine
(Netherlands/UK)
Mr. & Mrs. T Cocktail Mix (UK)
Munch 'ems Snack Food (UK)
Murata Electronics (Japan)
Myer's Original Rum (Canada)

N

NEC Computers (Japan)
Nakamichi Audio Equipment
(Japan)
National Electronics (Japan)
National Wax (UK)
Nature's Remedy Laxative (UK)
Naya Water (Canada)
Neet Hair Remover (UK)
Neosporin Ointment (UK)
Nescafe Coffee (Switzerland)
Nestea Tea (Switzerland)
Nestlé's Chocolate (Switzerland)
New American Library Books
(UK)
N'ice Sore Throat Spray (UK)
Night Nurse Cold Treatment
(UK)
Nikkei Index (Japan)

Nintendo Entertainment System
(Japan)
Nissan Motor Vehicles (Japan)
Nite Light Cold Treatment
(Switzerland)
Nivea Facial Cream (Germany)
Noilly Prat Vermouth (France)
Norelco Appliances
(Netherlands)
Noritake Dinnerware (Japan)
North Face Apparel (Hong Kong)
Norweigan Cruise (Norway)
Nutella Chocolate (Italy)
NuTone Appliances (UK)

O

Oasis Botled Water (France)
Ocean Spray Fruit Drinks (UK)
Oh Henry! Candy (Switzerland)
O'Keefe Ale (Canada)
Oki Electronics (Japan)
Old Charter Whiskey (UK)
Old Peculiar Ale (England)
Old Thompson Whiskey (UK)
Oleg Cassini Manicure (UK)
Olympus Photographic
Equipment (Japan)
Omega Watches (Switzerland)
Omni Hotels (Hong Kong)
One-A-Day Vitamins (Germany)
100 Grand Candy (Switzerland)
Onkyo Stereo Equipment (Japan)
Oodles Of Noodles Soup (Japan)
Opium Perfume (France)
Orafix Denture Adhesives (UK)
Orange Crush Soft Drink (UK)
Orangina Soft Drink (France)
Oregon Farms Frozen Baked
Goods (Canada)
The Original Lime-A-Way
Cleanser (Germany)
Ovaltine Mixes (Switzerland)
Owl Books (Germany)
Oxy Acne Treatment (UK)

P

Paco Rabanne Cologne (Spain)

Paloma Picasso Fragrance (Switzerland)

Pam Non-stick Cooking Spray (UK)

Panama Cigars (UK)

Panasonic Electronics (Japan)

Parker Pens (UK)

Park'n'Shop (Hong Kong)

Parents Magazine (Germany)

Passport Scotch (Scotland)

Patek Philippe Watches (Switzerland)

Payday Candy (Finland)

Peanut Butter Crunchers Candy (Finland)

Pearle Vision Centers (UK)

Pears Soap (UK)

Penguin Books (UK)

Pentax Photographic Equipment (Japan)

Pentel Writing Instruments (Japan)

Peoples Drug Store (Canada)

Pepsodent Dental-care Products (Netherlands/UK)

Perform Pet Food (Switzerland)

Pergamon Press (UK)

Perrier Sparkling Water (Switzerland)

Perugia Dinnerware (Italy)

Perugina Chocolate (Switzerland)

Peter Pan Playthings (UK)

Peter Pan Seafoods (Japan)

Peter Stuyvesant Cigarettes (UK)

Philco Electronics (Netherlands)

Philips Light Bulbs (Netherlands)

Pillsbury Dough (UK)

Pilot Pens (Japan)

Pilsner Urquell Beer (Czechoslovakia)

Pine Bros. Throat Drops (Finland)

Pioneer Electronics (Japan)

Pizzarias Snack Food (UK)

Playmate Toys (Hong Kong)

Plentitude Skin Care (France)

Plume Books (UK)

Poland Springs Mineral Water (Switzerland)

Polo By Ralph Lauren Fragrance (Switzerland)

Polydor Records (Netherlands)

Polygram Records (Netherlands)

Pond's Cold Cream (Netherlands/UK)

Popov Vodka (UK)

Popsicle Flavored Ice (Netherlands/UK)

Popular Photography Magazine (France)

Porsche Automobiles (Germany)

Poulan/Weed Eater Chainsaws (Sweden)

Power & Motoryacht Magazine (UK)

Prentice-Hall Books (UK)

ProStaff Tennis Racket (Finland)

Princess Cruises (UK)

Prince Matchabelli Toiletries (Netherlands/UK)

Prince Tennis Equipment (Italy)

Promise Margarine (Netherlands/UK)

Publisher's Weekly Magazine (UK)

Pulsar Watches (Japan)

Puma Athletic Footwear (Germany)

Pure & Simple Lotion (UK)

Push-Ups Ice Cream (Switzerland)

Q

Q-Tips Cotton Swabs (Netherlands/UK)

Quasar Electronics (Japan)

Quik Cocoa Mixes (Switzerland)

R

RCA Consumer Electronics (France)

Rado Watches (Switzerland)

Ragu Sauces (Netherlands/UK)

Raisinets Candy (Switzerland)

Raleigh Bicycles (Luxembourg)

Raleigh Cigarettes (UK)

Ralph Lauren Safari Fragrance (Switzerland)

Ralph's Supermarket (Canada)

Ramada Renaissance Inns (UK)

Ramses Condoms (UK)

Range Rover All-terrain Vehicle (UK)

Rave Hair Products (Netherlands/UK)

Ready Crust Pies (UK)

Red Cheek Apple Juice (UK)

Red Stripe Beer (Jamaica)

Regal Crown Sour Candies (UK)

Relska Vodka (UK)

Remy Martin Cognac (France)

Revell Models (UK)

Richland Cigarettes (UK)

Rich's Department Store (Canada)

Ricoh Photocopying/Facsimile (Japan)

Ricola Cough Drops (Switzerland)

Rinso Detergent (Netherlands/UK)

Rive Gauche Fragrance (France)

Road and Track Magazine (France)

Roland Musical Equipment (Japan)

Rolex Watches (Switzerland)

Rolling Rock Beer (Canada)

Rolls-Royce Automobiles (UK)

Ronrico Rum (Canada)

Rose's Lime Juice (UK)

Rossignol Ski Equipment (France)

Rothmans Cigarettes (UK)

Royal Caribbean Cruise Line (Norway)

Royal Doulton Fine China (UK)

Roy Rogers Fast-food Franchise (Canada)

Royal Viking Cruise Lines (Norway)

RR Bowker Reference Books (UK)

Rug Fresh Rug Deodorizer (UK)

Rusty Scupper Restaurant Chain (Switzerland)

S

SAAB Automobiles (Sweden)

SBK Records (UK)

Sail Magazine (UK)

Saks Fifth Avenue (Bahrain)

Sambuca Romana (Italy)

Samsung Electronics (Korean)

Samuel Smith's Ale (England)

Samyang Cup Ramen Soup (South Korea)

Sani-Flush (UK)

Sansui (Japan)

Sanyo Fisher (Japan)

Sapporo Beer (Japan)

Saratoga Springs Water (France)

Sauza Tequila (Mexico)

Savarin Coffee (UK)

Schick Electric Razors (Netherlands)

Schrafft's Chocolates (UK)

Schweppes Soft Drinks (UK)

Scientific American Magazine (Germany)

Scripto Mighty Match Lighter (Japan)

Scrub Free Cleanser (Germany)

Sea & Ski Suntan Lotion (Netherlands/UK)

Sega/Genesis Video Entertainment System (Japan)

Seiko Watches (Japan)

Seagram's Gin (Canada)

Seagram's VO Whiskey (Canada)

7-Eleven Convenience Stores (Japan)

Shalimar Fragrance (France)

Sharp Electronics (Japan)

Sharwood's Spices (UK)

Shaws Supermarkets (UK)

Sheaffer Pens (Switzerland)

Shedd's Country Crock Margarine (UK)

Shell Oil (Netherlands)

Shield Soap (Netherlands/UK)

Shine On (Netherlands/UK)

Shiseido Cosmetics (Japan)

Showboats International (France)

Siemens Electronics (Germany)

Sierra Designs Apparel (Hong Kong)

Signal Mouthwash (Netherlands)

Signet Books (UK)

Sine-Off Sleep Aid (UK)

Singer Sewing Machines (Hong Kong)

Singha Beer (Thailand)

Sinkmaster (Sweden)

Sir Walter Raleigh Tobacco (UK)

Skol Lager (England)

Slow Fe Iron (Switzerland)

Smash Records (Netherlands)

Smith Corona Typewriters (UK)

Smith & Wesson Guns (UK)

Sno Caps Candy (Switzerland)

Snuggle Detergent (Netherlands/UK)

So Fine Hair Conditioner (Germany)

Soho Natural Sodas (Canada)

Sominex Sleep Aid (UK)

Sony Electronics (Japan)

Sorrento Cheese (France)

S.O.S. Soap Pads (Germany)

Spalding Sporting Goods (Venezuela)

Spark's Tune-Up Centers (UK)

Spartus Clocks (UK)

Spice Islands Spices (Australia)

Spiegels Catalog (Germany)

Spray 'n Vac Rug Cleaners (UK)

Standard Oil (UK)

Star Brand Olive Oil (Spain)

Steinlager Beer (Germany)

Stereo Review Magazine (France)

Stern's Department Store (Canada)

St. Moritz Cigarettes (UK)

St. Pauli Girl Beer (Germany)

Stock Vermouth (Italy)

Stoned Wheat Thins (Canada)

Stouffer Frozen Entrees (Switzerland)

Stroehmann Sunbeam Baked Goods (Canada)

Subaru Automobiles (Japan)

Sucrets Cough Surpressant (UK)

Sudafed Cold Treatment (UK)

Sunkist Fun Fruit Snacks (Netherlands/UK)

Sunkist Soda (UK)

Sunkist Vitamin C (Switzerland)

Sunlight Soap (Netherlands/UK)

Suntory Beer (Japan)

Sunrise Coffee (Switzerland)

Surf Detergent (Netherlands/UK)

Suzuki Motor Vehicles (Japan)

Swatch Watches (Switzerland)

Swiss Army Knife (Switzerland)

Swish Toilet Bowl Cleanser (UK)

Swisscare Soap (France)

Switzer Licorice Bites (Finland)

Sylvania Electronics (Netherlands)

T

TDK Tape (Japan)

TNT Overland Express (Australia)

TV Guide (Australia)

Tabby Cat Food (UK)

Tanqueray Gin (England)

Tappan Ranges (Sweden)

Taster's Choice Coffee
(Switzerland)

Taylor Made Golf Apparel
(France)

TEAC Electronics (Japan)

Tecate Beer (Mexico)

Technics Electronics (Japan)

Ten High Whiskey (England)

10-K Soft Drink (Japan)

Tetley's Tea (UK)

Tetra Min Flake Food (Germany)

The Body Shop (UK)

The Famous Grouse Scotch
(Scotland)

Theraflu Cold Treatment
(Switzerland)

Thermos Appliances (Japan)

Tic Tacs Candy (Italy)

Tigress Fragrance
(Netherlands/UK)

Tio Sancho Mexican Foods
(Netherlands/UK)

Toblerone Chocolate
(Switzerland)

Toledo Scales (Switzerland)

Toll House Crackers
(Switzerland)

Tommy Armour Golf Equipment
(UK)

Top-Flite Golf Balls (Venezuela)

Tops Supermarkets
(Netherlands)

Toshiba Electronics (Japan)

Totino's Pizza (UK)

Tourneau Watches (Switzerland)

Town House Crackers (UK)

Toyota Automobiles (Japan)

Travelodge Hotels (UK)

Travel Weekly Magazine (UK)

Tree Top Fruit Drinks
(Netherlands/UK)

Tretorn Footwear (Sweden)

Triaminic (Switzerland)

TropWorld Casino (Hong Kong)

Tropicana Juices (Canada)

Truckstop Corporation of
American (UK)

Tsingtao Beer (China)

Tube Rose Tobacco (UK)

Tuff Gong Records (Netherlands)

Tums Antacid (UK)

20th Century Fox Film Studios
(Australia)

20 Mule Team Borax (UK)

Twinings Tea (UK)

Twirl Chocolate Bar (UK)

U

Uniroyal/Goodrich Tires (France)

Universal Furniture (Hong Kong)

Universal Gym Equipment (UK)

Universal Matches (Sweden)

Universal Pictures (Japan)

Universal Studios Hollywood
(Japan)

Universal Studios Florida
(Japan)

Uptons Supermarket
(Netherlands)

Uptown Records (Japan)

V

Value Rent-a-Car Rental (Japan)

Van de Kamp's Frozen Foods
(UK)

Vaseline Intensive Care
(Netherlands/UK)

Variety Magazine (UK)

Verve Records (Netherlands)

Verve Hair Care
(Netherlands/UK)

Viceroy Cigarettes (UK)

Victor Records (Japan)

Viking Books (UK)

Viking Sewing Machines (Sweden)

Villeroy and Boch Tableware (Germany)

Virgin Records (UK)

Vital-Perfection Skin Care (Japan)

Vittel Water (Switzerland)

Vivarin Anti-Sleep (UK)

Volkswagen Automobiles (Germany)

Volvic Water (France)

Volvo Automobiles (Sweden)

Vuarnet (France)

W

Wasa Crispbread (Switzerland)

Waterford Glass (UK)

Watney's Ale (England)

Watson's Personal Care Stores (Hong Kong)

Weetabix Cereal (UK)

Wella Balsam Hair-care Products (Germany)

Werther's Original Candy (Germany)

Whirlaway Appliances (Sweden)

White Diamonds Fragrance (Netherlands/UK)

White Horse Whiskey (UK)

White Shoulders Fragrance (Netherlands/UK)

Whoppers Candy (Finland)

Wild Turkey Whiskey (France)

Wilkinson Blades (Switzerland)

William's Mug Shaving Soap (UK)

Willy Wonka Candy (Switzerland)

Wilson Sporting Goods (Finland)

Winchell's Donut House (Canada)

Wish-Bone Salad Dressing (Netherlands/UK)

Wisk Detergent (Netherlands/UK)

Wizard Charcoal Lighter (UK)

Woman's Day Magazine (France)

Woman's World Magazine (Germany)

Woolite Bleach (UK)

Wyborowa Vodka (Canada)

Wyler's Lemonade (UK)

Y

Yale Locks (UK)

Yamaha Musical Instruments (Japan)

Yardley of London Soap (Germany)

Yogplait Yogurt (France)

Yokohama Tires (Japan)

Yonex Electronics (Japan)

Yoo Hoo Soft Drink (France)

Yugo Automobiles (Yugoslavia)

Yves St. Laurent Perfume (France)

Z

Zagnut Candy Bar (Finland)

Zenith Computers (France)

Zephyr Hill Water (France)

Zerex Antifreeze (Germany)

Zero Candy Bar (Finland)

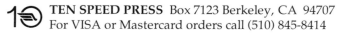